CONQUEST OF WORLD HUNGER AND POVERTY

CONQUEST OF WORLD

HUNGER AND POVERTY

DOUGLAS ENSMINGER
PAUL BOMANI

THE IOWA STATE UNIVERSITY PRESS / AMES

TO **MAHATMA GANDHI** AND **MARTIN LUTHER KING, JR.**

Douglas Ensminger, Professor of Rural Sociology at the University of Missouri, was formerly Ford Foundation representative for India and Pakistan, 1951–1953, and for India and Nepal, 1953–1970.

Paul Bomani, Ambassador of Tanzania to the United States, was formerly Tanzanian Minister for Agriculture and Cooperatives, 1960–1962; Minister for Finance, 1962–1965; and Minister for Economic Affairs and Development Planning, 1965–1970.

Composed and printed by The Iowa State University Press, Ames Iowa 50010

First edition, 1980

Library of Congress Cataloging in Publication Data
Ensminger, Douglas
    Conquest of world hunger and poverty.

    Includes bibliographies and index.
    1. Underdeveloped areas—Agriculture. 2. Underdeveloped areas—Food supply.
3. International economic relations. I. Bomani, P., 1925–   joint author. II. Title.
HD1417.E57   338.1′9′1724   80–10762
ISBN 0–8138–1140–6

CONTENTS

PREFACE

Two world leaders, Robert S. McNamara, President of the World Bank, and Dr. Julius Nyerere, President of Tanzania, have challenged the continuation of development policies and strategies that perpetuate poverty. President Nyerere forcefully predicts that if changes to alleviate the plight of the poor do not come from established political leadership and institutions, they will surely come from the people who have been denied an opportunity to earn a living and to live free from the fear of hunger.

Robert S. McNamara, addressing the board of governors of the World Bank at its annual meeting in Nairobi, Kenya, on September 24, 1973, commented on the increasingly critical situation for the world's poor in concrete terms:

Despite a decade of unprecedented increase in national products of developing countries, the poorest segments of their populations have received little benefits. Nearly 800 million individuals—40 percent out of a total of two billion—survive on incomes (in U.S. purchasing power) of 30 cents per day in conditions of malnutrition, illiteracy, and squalor. They are suffering poverty in absolute terms.

The political implications of unrelieved poverty and the inevitability of change were the subjects of a sensitive analysis by Dr. Nyerere in his address before the Royal Commonwealth Society in London, in November 1975:

The problem of poverty, and of the national dependency and humiliation which goes with it, will be tackled at its root when the endless pursuit of economic growth for the sake of growth ceases to be the major objective of national and international policies. The objective must be the eradication of poverty and the establishment of a minimum standard of living for all people.

Tackling the problem of poverty in the world is first and foremost a matter of political will and determination. . . . But the question as the poor see it is not whether there should be changes in the present economic situation; changes will come one way or the other. The question is when, how, they will be brought about.

This book relates world hunger to world poverty by examining the methods used by individuals, institutions, and nations in acquiring control over production resources. It points out the implications of their persistence in depriving the world's poor of an opportunity to earn enough to meet basic human needs. With few exceptions, the policies and development strategies followed by the developing countries have contributed to the emergence of an elitist culture alongside a culture of poverty. In most of the developing countries two nations clearly are emerging within a single nation. This book stresses both national and international policies and program strategies that are essential for the removal of conditions that create poverty and hunger. It is optimistic in its outlook about the prospects of sharing resources, technology, and experience within the world community in order to improve the quality of life (level of living) for all people, especially the world's poor.

Our concern is to analyze the strategies and the time required to eliminate conditions that create poverty; to integrate the poor into the social, economic, and political fabric of the developing countries; to transform the traditional societies moving toward modernization; to provide all people with opportunities to work and earn enough to meet basic needs; and to improve the quality of life for all people.

The two underlying messages to be drawn from *Conquest of World Hunger and Poverty* are: industrialized developed countries should examine, with a sense of urgency and a fresh perspective, their foreign policies, interests, and commitments to the developing countries of the world; and the developing countries should recognize that unattended mass poverty is the breeding ground for discontent, political instability, uprisings, and revolutions.

Following World War II, the United States and the European community joined in a foreign policy of economic and military aid for the reconstruction of Europe and thereby contained the spread of communism. While we can acknowledge the success story of reconstruction, it is clear that the same cannot be said about the containment of communism, for this still remains an unfinished task. Needed now are commitments to eradicate poverty and abolish the fear of hunger.

Given the magnitude of world hunger, poverty, population, and energy issues, and their unattended implications for political instability, uprisings, and revolutions, the present challenge and need is for strong foreign policy statements offering assistance to the developing countries that are committed to ending the conditions that have created poverty, thereby raising the standard of living for all peoples, particularly the poorest of the poor.

ACKNOWLEDGMENTS

The book draws heavily on the authors' intimate knowledge of the cultures and three decades of development experience in Africa and Southeast Asia, as well as a working knowledge of developing countries in the Middle East and Central and South America, in addition to the authors' familiarity with much of the literature written about developing countries. Therefore, it is not possible to identify and give credit to any one individual or source for the ideas developed in this study. What is important is to acknowledge the world's hungry and poor, about whom this book is written, have been the force compelling the authors to write on their behalf.

Mention must be made of the contributions of Katy Douglass Arnac and Jenny Shearin in coordinating the library resource references, supervising the initial layout, and preliminary editing of the manuscript. Thanks are due to Don Pierce and Allan Valla Bomani for their painstaking library research and to Carolyn Spieckermann Schumann and Rosalind Murray for typing the manuscript.

Very special thanks are extended to Suzanne Lowitt of the Iowa State University Press and to the professional staff of the press for the care associated with all aspects of publication.

Special thanks also to our wives, Hildegard Bomani and Mary Ensminger, for the inspiration they gave us in writing this book.

Douglas Ensminger and Paul Bomani

INTRODUCTION

Poverty is the warehouse for hunger. Both endanger world peace and security and are major subjects for all-level international and national discussion. They are basically not the problem of insufficient resources or lack of technology to harness and utilize existing resources for human use and consumption. Certainly the problem does not arise from the absence of potentialities required to meet the challenge, or the scarcity of land for development and production, or shortage of capital for the necesssary investments, or difficulties of expertise and essential labor for the kind of work involved. It is none of such impediments nor, indeed, in the final analysis, human's inability to extricate themselves from adverse conditions of life which threaten their existence. We have always been able either to adjust and adapt ourselves to new situations or change them accordingly to suit our needs. Wherein then lie the problems of poverty and hunger?

In a nutshell, the problem of humankind's own reluctance to face unpleasant facts is our delayed action to reality. This is usually embedded in a misguided and often selfish concept of security and development or progress. It emerges and manifests itself in a subsequent failure to recognize the obvious need for and inescapable demands of the nations and peoples of the world to live together in peace and harmony. The result is the present chaotic scramble for priorities in which greater damage than good is done to humanity as a whole. And when we conveniently or unwittingly permit ourselves to be stampeded by false ideas; when society allows itself to be swamped by evil promptings of exploitation for political, economic, or social gains; and when nations let themselves be dragged through the mire of greed or wanton fear, then reason is lost and illusion takes over.

No topic has of recent years been discussed more intensively than poverty and hunger; no subject has enjoyed greater publicity and unanimity; yet the urgent and imperative political, economic, social, and human need to solve the problem remains undiminished. If anything, it is on the increase. But the problem must be tackled and equitably solved. Let the world seriously take the cue from the poor wallowing in the squalor and misery of their grinding poverty and agonizing hunger. Either the affluent adapt themselves to the inevitable, in which case they determine the direction and control the tempo of the change that must be, or face the tide that must of necessity sweep and crash them to submission, probably destroying all in the process. I recommend *Conquest of World Hunger and Poverty* in the belief that it may help jolt the conscience into conscientious action on the subject.

His Excellency Al-haj Aboud M. Jumbe, M.B.M.
Vice-President
United Republic of Tanzania
State House, Zanzibar
Tanzania

CONQUEST OF WORLD HUNGER AND POVERTY

For us today there can be no sacrifice higher than to forget distinctions of high and low and realize the equality of all men.—**Mahatma Gandhi**

True peace is not merely the absence of tension but it is the presence of justice in brotherhood.—**Martin Luther King, Jr.**

1

THE ELITE VS THE POOR

The great issue of our age is not the Iron Curtain or the Bamboo Screen. Rather it is hunger and poverty, made dramatically apparent by the enormous and constantly widening gap separating the 450 million well-nourished inhabitants of the world from the 1.3 billion who are malnourished because they lack the minimum essentials of life and are deprived of the opportunity to work and earn enough to meet minimum human needs, including access to production resources.

COLONIAL EMPIRES. Greed, quest for world power, and control over the world's resources were dominating influences resulting in the creation of colonial empires The framework for institutionalizing colonialism was the exploitation of resources for the improvement of the colonial powers, not development of resources for the advancement of the people within the colonies.

When colonialism declined, an immediate power vacuum occurred within the new independent nations. Filling this power vacuum were the elite groups (political, economic, and, quite frequently, military) having as their central objective the control of the countries' finances, minerals, land, and water for self-enrichment. In some cases the process was orderly while in others there were uprisings, even warring factions. But the elite have behaved toward their own poor in much the same way the colonial powers behaved. The poor people, most of whom are rural, have been denied equal access to the countries' development resources, and they have been exploited for the betterment of those who control the resources. The elite power structure, with its deep roots in the colonial era, today dominates the developing countries' policies and development strategies and, like the former colonial officers, the elite have little feeling for the poor.

It was inevitable that the elite power structure developed under colonial rule would continue to thrive under new, independent, and self-governing nations (now called developing countries). The elite wanted freedom from colonial rule, but they did not want within-country revolutionary reforms. They wanted to be rid of the colonial rulers, and at the same time, keep their wealth and power.

Under colonial rule, the poor, hungry, unemployed, illiterate, and destitute people in developing countries were accepted in much the same way one accepts vast acreages of desert land as being poor. They were not seen as miserable human beings living without hope.

Under colonial rule, the colonial powers put a premium on agricultural products for export and ignored food-crop agriculture. The same priorities exist in most of the developing countries today. Earning foreign exchange has a higher priority than increasing production of food crops to meet human needs.

While there was internal strife as many new nations emerged, the fighting was always between competing power structures. Independence from foreign rule was achieved, but the poor did not gain freedom from poverty.

As the elite began to govern, instead of legislating land and institutional reforms, they adopted policies and supported development programs that were designed to strengthen their hold over the economy and development resources and to reinforce their positions as political leaders. In the developed countries the middle class exercise considerable constraint over the elite. The absence of a middle class and the lack of political influence by the poor in the developing countries allow the elite to function without restraints.

Yet it would be wrong to imply that all who can be classified as elitist are immoral and indifferent to the poor. Many leading industrialists and financiers are concerned humanitarians. One can often find people who have control over vast resources following policies that assure employees of an income sufficient to meet basic human needs, and provide retirement benefits and security in old age. Often those who press the hardest for reforms to benefit the poor come from the elitist group.

However, the truth must prevail; the majority of the elite are exploitive and resist reforms. However, they are beginning to see that change is inevitable, and the winds of change show that the people will eventually win out in their demands for greater access to production resources and opportunities for employment.

Wisdom is needed at this time in world history to provide guidance to create conditions for a more just and equitable society. Continuation of the status quo—the elite minority exploiting the poor majority—should no longer be tolerated. At the same time we must reject the idea that the only way to bring about a just society is through revolutionary methods that destroy the elite and free the resources for the masses. Such revolutionary tactics can only result in a strong, centrally dominated government that will regulate and dominate the lives of all.

A third alternative should be examined with great care by both the elite and the poor. It involves change through institutional and governmental processes. When confronted with the inevitability of change, the elite will gain by pledging support for reforms that assure them enough resources to live comfortably and at the same time enable them to create conditions for a more humane, just, and sustainably free society.

The final message is that the elite must be rescued from continuing their position of dominance and denying the poor an opportunity to earn enough to live as self-respecting human beings. They will need assistance in changing their role from exploiters to supporters of revolutionary land, resource, and institutional reforms.

The two issues likely to determine whether we will have a future generation of peace are first, whether or not the elite-dominated political power structures in developing countries conclude it is in their interest to support land and institutional reforms, making production resources more equitably available to the masses living in poverty; and second, how the nations that have acquired wealth choose to share and assist the poor developing countries.

By sharing, all will gain. Democratic institutions will survive and be strengthened, and the survival of the human race will be assured.

Since the elite and the poor now constitute two separate cultures in most, if not all, developing countries, and are increasingly functioning as two separate nations within each single developing nation, drastic changes in national policies followed by bold and innovative development strategies will be required to integrate the poor into the social, economic, and political fabric of the developing countries.

The achievement of a minimum acceptable quality of life for all the people in developing countries will be difficult, time consuming, costly, and frustrating, but it is important to maintain faith that this is an attainable goal. One cannot read the record of the past thirty years of development experience and be pessimistic about the future if developing countries will provide the policies and unwavering political leadership, and if the developed nations accept a strong supportive role in making available resources to carry out revolutionary reform programs. These are two big "ifs," but the potential to achieve is undeniably present.

WESTERN INDUSTRIALISM. It would be wrong to argue against profit motives which have fired the engines and provided the motivation for the high level of living of the great majority of the people in Western industrialized nations. But it is not improper to question the Western industrialized nations' profit motives when operationally they exploit the poor developing countries. All too frequently the motivation of Western industrialized nations has been based on what could be sold at the maximum profit. Producing to meet human needs has been of secondary concern.

With few exceptions, the industrialized aid-giving nations failed to understand the depth of commitment that freedom fighters had made to improve the living conditions of their poor once they were free. Given the advances in science and technology, the industrialized nations naturally felt if the tradition-bound developing countries were to progress, they could do so only by giving up their traditional ways and beliefs and by taking full advantage of science and technology, which was nonpolitical and available to the world community.

It was also the contention of the aid-giving nations that initially they could not afford to commit substantial funds on programs to improve the living conditions of the poor. "Too much expenditure on social overhead," argued the Western economists. We see, therefore, that the developing countries were encouraged by the aid policy decision makers to move development emphasis away from programs that would improve the living conditions of the rural poor to capital-intensive projects. These projects, in turn, were expected to add to the wealth of the country and create within-country sources of revenue for new investments. All this was expected to provide future employment opportunities; eventually, the unemployed poor would be brought into the development process and advance.

It was not that the developing countries' political leaders were callous about the needs of their poor people in opting to follow the industrialized nations' development model. Rather, it is a case of the political leaders' lack of development experience, their desire to make progress quickly, and their expectations that advances in science and technology would make possible many shortcuts in the development process.

For whatever reasons one wishes to support the developing countries' decision to follow the model of the industrialized nations, the evidence from thirty years of development experience is that it was the wrong model.

While that conclusion may be harsh, it may also be reasonable to conclude that developing countries might have had greater success had they not been assisted by the advanced industrialized nations. To have been assisted by industrialized nations to carry out their own conceived programs, which were early oriented to improving the conditions of the poor, would have been one thing. But what happened was that with increasing pressure using economic aid as the lever, the aid-giving nations played a dominant role in moving the developing countries toward capital-intensive investments and industrialization.

In cultural terms, one can say the industrialized Western nations have looked at the developing nations through the Western vantage point of materialism. They perceived that the only way the poor, wretched masses of people in the developing countries could achieve a level of living comparable to the West was for them to follow the Western model.

Political leaders in the developing countries early found their future was best assured by being supportive of programs that benefited those in control of the country's finances, land, and institutions. Therefore, it did not take much persuasion from the aid-giving nations to shift political and developmental emphasis from the poor to capital-intensive projects and industrialization.

One may ask, What do the poor expect out of life? An equally important question, if not the most important, is what level of living will be culturally acceptable and economically achievable for all people?

The evidence is clear that the materialistic level of living, which was the model for achievement over the past thirty years, is out of reach economically and would not be culturally satisfying to the poor whose immediate concern is survival with a sense of security.

It is important to establish first a minimum level of living before stating what would be acceptable culturally and economically for the millions now living in poverty. Once this minimum has been achieved, a higher level of living can then be viewed as attainable.

The minimum essential elements in a level of living that seem likely to be culturally acceptable and economically achievable by the masses of poor people within the time frame of three human generations can be stated as follows:

1. All who are able to work should have an opportunity to earn enough to meet minimum family needs, with first priority on an adequately nutritious diet.

2. Minimum essential health services should be available to all people, and sanitary conditions should be supportive of good health.

3. Education should be for all the people, oriented toward teaching people to live more fully and to be more effective in earning a liv-

ing. Education should be continuous and not confined to formal schooling.

4. All should have housing that meets climatic conditions.

5. All should have pure water available.

6. There should be time for leisure and participation in value-oriented cultural programs.

7. There should be a sense of achievement, fulfillment, and economic and social well-being.

The achievement of this minimum level of living will provide a sense of fulfillment and much needed security for all the world's people.

DEVELOPMENT OBJECTIVES: MEETING BASIC NEEDS. Meeting basic human needs—food, health, shelter, clothing, education, and employment—which are all prerequisites for human dignity, should have the first call on the world's resources.

While volumes have been written and millions of words have been spoken by political leaders about the plight of the poor and the need to improve their level of living, few can match the government of China's claim that its 650 million peasants have achieved an acceptable level of living. However, while they have approached the problem differently from mainland China, Israel and Taiwan have succeeded also in raising the level of living of all sectors of their populations.

Tanzania, an East African country, is one among few developing nations (committed to democratic methods) to make an unqualified attempt to improve the quality of life for all people; to follow through with policies and programs; to involve all people in development; and to assure that all benefit from development.

It is significant that when Tanzania gained its independence in 1961 it initially followed what had become the traditional way of organizing a government into ministries of education, agriculture, industry, planning, and finance, and supported the development initiative of individuals who possessed resources and managerial acumen.

During those first three years of Tanzania's independence, President Julius K. Nyerere continuously toured the new nation, talking, listening, and observing the implications of a multipolicy system that persistently divided the country on issues. President Nyerere also observed the individual entrepreneurs whose primary motivation was to make money through exploiting the poor. It did not take long for him to see that the current development in Tanzania would enrich a few and impoverish 85 percent of the country's people, barring any hope that independence could be superior to colonial rule.

Through President Nyerere's leadership and his power of persuasion, the three political parties merged into one national party, the Tanganyika African National Union (TANU), renamed in 1977 the Tanzania Revolutionary Party (Chama Cha Mapinduzi). During the three years that President Nyerere spent touring the country, talking and listening to people, he and the people of Tanzania evolved a development philosophy. The new national development objectives placed the national political party and the government in support of far-reaching changes, designed and directed toward achieving a higher and more secure quality of life for all.

Tanzania's new development objectives were set forth in the Arusha Declaration which states:

1. All human beings are equal.
2. Every individual has a right to dignity and respect.
3. Every citizen is an integral part of the nation and has the right to take an equal part in government at the local, regional, and national level.
4. Every citizen has the right to freedom of expression, of movement, or religious belief and of association within the context of the law.
5. Every individual has the right to receive from society protection of his life and property held according to law.
6. Every individual has the right to receive a just return for his labor.
7. All citizens together possess all the natural resources of the country in trust for their descendants.
8. In order to ensure economic justice the state must have effective control over the principal means of production.
9. It is the responsibility of the state to intervene actively in the economic life of the nation to ensure the well-being of all citizens and to prevent the exploitation of one person by another or one group by another, so as to prevent the accumulation of wealth which is inconsistent with the existence of a classless society.

Few people have campaigned more openly on behalf of the poor than the father of India's independence, Mahatma Gandhi. Gandhi knew only too well that the masses of India's people, most of whom were rural, were poor not because they were incapable of development as human beings, but rather because the elite denied them an opportunity to be productive and refused access to institutions and services.

Instead of advocating policies and programs to destroy the power structure that so firmly controlled the nation's land, wealth, and institutions, Gandhi's approach was to recognize that poor people were

India's greatest potential resource for development. Gandhi held to the view that as the masses of poor people were developed as human beings, India's human resources would, in turn, contribute to the building of the new nation. According to Gandhi, the exploitation of the poor could be ended not by the sheer physical destruction of a few rich people, but by removing the ignorance of the poor and teaching them to be noncooperative with their exploiters.

It is the advancement of the developing countries' human resources which must be central to all national policies and development strategies, within a national commitment to improve the quality of life for all the people.

The evidence is indisputable that all development takes place through people and people's institutions. If the objective is to augment the rate and quality of development, it follows that the emphasis must be on the people and their institutions.

Since all development takes place through people, an unquestionable conclusion, drawn from the past thirty years of experience is that the maximum benefits from programs designed to improve the quality of life will be realized only as the people who are to benefit are full, active, and continuous participants in all phases of development. This means the people must be involved in the initial discussions. It must be the people's decision to want to improve and support changes. And to implement programs, they must be involved in the planning and leadership.

Whereas capital-intensive programs, which have dominated the development strategy the past two decades, have been planned from the top, quality of life programs must be planned from the people's level, or the bottom. Improving quality of life must increasingly come to mean achieving a level of living that will be culturally acceptable and economically feasible for all.

Although each culture will have a different conception of what constitutes an acceptable level of living, improving the quality of nutrition for all people must be the central and immediate goal. In the future, enough food must mean more than enough to meet market demands. Enough food must take on new meaning. It should encompass the demand for minimum nutritional requirements for all people.

It would be a mistake to place the primary emphasis on nutrition when defining quality of life, without recognizing that the basic reason for malnutrition is lack of income. The nutritional requirements of the poor with per capita incomes of less than $100 a year cannot be met at the marketplace.

Differentiation should be made between objectives and means.

Within a national policy to improve the quality of life, achieving an adequate diet is the objective. Employment opportunities to earn enough for a nutritionally adequate diet is an essential means for making this possible for all people.

Improving the quality of nutrition is one of the surest ways to improve the health of all. The delivery of health services for all people must be one of the essential elements present in an improved quality of life and the achievement of a minimum adequate nutrition obviously will contribute to buildng and maintaining healthy bodies and alert minds.

Within the national policies designed to improve the quality of life for all, which were pointed out earlier, one essential means of achieving a minimum adequate diet was to provide opportunities for everyone to work and earn. It was also shown that in shifting the development strategy to improving the quality of life, there was a move away from capital-intensive development strategy to labor-intensive strategy. While the first essential policy for a labor-intensive strategy must be to provide employment, the quality and quantity of labor output will be directly related to all laborers having adequate nutrition for a labor-intensive program.

In examining the past thirty years of the developing countries' experience, one finds all too few references relating family values to achieving program objectives. While there has been considerable speculation about the relationship between family level of living and family size, definitive research is lacking.

It is sobering to understand that the dominant value of millions of landless laborers throughout the developing countries is freedom from the fear of hunger. An Indian peasant expressed the most important value of the landless laborers when he said, "My wish in life is just to have enough to eat, nothing more."

It is known from worldwide development experience that when programs for improving the level of living of the poor sector have been formulated by national planners and imposed on the people, the expected response of the families to accept and integrate the new into the family values has been disappointing. In any approach to improving the level of living of the poor, it must be appreciated that the circumstances of those living in poverty determine their dominant and persistent value *to survive if they can*. It seems reasonable to conclude that only as those living in poverty achieve their dominant value—assurance of survival—will they then see the potential to improve their level of living.

Once accepted, family values—how they are expressed, how new values replace old ones, and how they are set in motion for change—must be built into national policies to improve the quality of life. These values will be the determinants in setting the pace and in eventually improving the level of living of everyone. It is impossible to overstate the difference between the existing value to survive, if they can, and the value to improve the quality of life. The improved quality of life value is presently foreign to those locked in poverty.

It is one thing for planners to understand the relationship between population growth and the nation's resources and foresee the difficulties of improving family levels of living and quite another for the families to see beyond their immediate concerns, all related to survival.

Since the "top-down" approach (initiated at the national level and then imposed upon the people) to educate, persuade, and motivate couples to limit procreation has brought only a qualified response from those living in poverty, it seems obvious that a new strategy is needed. Awareness of the value of a small family will likely come about in the process of the value shift from survival to improving the level of living, but only when all national policies and programs are supportive of families and when families experience new opportunities that change their lives. And since improving the quality of life development strategy is emerging out of the past thirty years of developing countries' experience, it seems reasonable to forecast that, at least for the next several decades, quality of life, not gross national product, will be the criterion for measuring progress in the developing countries.

To evaluate progress in improving quality of life will be a formidable task. It will require interdisciplinary research involving sociology, cultural anthropology, psychology, economics, and political science.

It will be mandatory for political leaders, planners, administrators, and evaluators to understand that a national commitment to improve the quality of life must be unqualified and continuous. Five-year plans should avoid setting targets that will be unachievable. Changes can be brought about with fewer tensions and less frustration if the development plans include a clarification of the ways these changes are to be accomplished.

If the journey is a thousand miles and the only way to get there is to walk, then the first step is the most important, for it is the beginning. So will be the developing countries' commitments to improve the quality of life for all. Policies that commit the nation to an improved quality of live will be vital for delivering all the people into the promised land, up and out of poverty.

REFERENCES

Borgstrom, Georg. *The Hungry Planet: The Modern World at the Edge of Famine.* London: Macmillan, 1967.

Kurien, C. T. *Poverty and Development.* Madras, India: Christian Literature Society, 1974.

McNamara, Robert S. Address to the Board of Governors of the World Bank, Nairobi, Kenya. Sept. 24, 1973. World Bank publication.

Mooneyham, W. Stanley. *What Do You Say to a Hungry World?* Waco, Tex.: World Books, 1975.

Myrdal, Gunnar. *Challenge to Affluence.* New York: Partheon Books, 1962.

Orr, John Boyd, and Lubbock, David. *The White Man's Dilemma.* London: George Allen & Unwin, 1964.

Power, Jonathan, and Holenstein, Anne-Marie. *World of Hunger: A Strategy for Survival.* London: Temple Smith, 1976.

President's National Advisory Commission on Rural Poverty. *Rural Poverty in the United States.* Washington, D.C.: USGPO, May 1968.

Rockefeller, John D., III. *The Second American Revolution: Some Personal Observations.* New York: Harper & Row, 1973.

Vallinatos, E. G. *Fear in the Countryside: The Control of Agricultural Resources in the Poor Countries by Nonpeasant Elites.* Cambridge, Md.: Ballinger, 1976.

2

OVERPOPULATION

The distinguished biologist and writer, Julian Huxley, in an essay commenting on the crisis of overpopulation (Fairfield Osborn, ed., *Our Crowded Planet: Essays on the Pressures of Population,* 1962), has cautioned:

Overpopulation is a world problem so serious as to override all other world problems, such as soil erosion, poverty, malnutrition, raw material shortages, illiteracy, even disarmament. The future of the whole human species is at stake. If nothing is done about it, in the next hundred years man will cease to have any claims to be the Lord of Creation or the controller of his own destiny, and will have become the cancer of his planet, uselessly devouring its resources and negating his own possibilities in a spite of overmultiplication.

The world's population, which reached 4.2 billion in 1978, was increasing at a rate of 1.9 percent per year up to 1970, when it fell to the present rate of 1.7 percent per year. Assuming the world's population rate continues at 1.7 percent per year, the world's population will double in forty-one years (2019).

With the world facing such a growth in population, the problem of poverty must be dealt with.

THE CULTURE OF POVERTY. While not enough is known about the people who are living in poverty, it is known that of the two billion citizens of developing countries, at least 40 percent, or 800 million, are living in subhuman conditions. Most of the developing countries' poor are rural residents and thus limited to earning their living from agriculture. Many of the rural poor who farm either have small fragmented holdings or are tenants whose landlords take the lion's share. At the bottom of the poverty heap are the landless laborers who work seasonally at very low wages. To be partially employed or unemployed is characteristic of the culture of poverty. The one difference between being in prison and being in poverty is that except for those with life sentences, those in prison know when they will get out. To be born in poverty is a life sentence—from the cradle to the grave.

The 800 million people in poverty live in continuous fear of hunger. They do not know how they will provide for their next meal, nor do they know when they will eat again. Their meager meals go first to the men, second to the children, and what is left goes to the women. They eat to survive; nutrition is not a part of their vocabulary.

Illiteracy among the poor is high, and they have benefited little from formal education. They live by tradition in the way they farm, work, and earn a living. They are isolated from the effects of government policies, programs, and institutions. There is nearly a complete void in an institutional delivery system for the poor. Folk medicine, not scientific medicine, is practiced among this segment of the population.

Unfortunately, political leaders, administrators, planners, and upper- and middle-class families in the developing countries generally cannot relate to the feelings of tenants with landlords who are forever threatening eviction and taking an inordinate share of the harvest.

To give meaning to what it is like to live in poverty, Robert Heilbroner (quoted in W. Stanley Mooneyham, *What Do You Say to a Hungry World?* 1975), takes a middle-class Canadian-American family and reduces its life-style to an existence equivalent to that of at least a billion poverty-ridden people in the developing countries. He then refashions the home and life-style of its occupants as it would be for people in developing countries who live under conditions of dire poverty.

1. Take out the furniture, except a few old blankets, a kitchen table and one chair.

2. Take away all the clothing, except for the oldest dress or suit for each member of the family, and a shirt or blouse. Leave one pair of shoes for the head of the family.

3. Empty the pantry and refrigerator except for a small bag of flour, some sugar and salt, a few moldy potatoes for tonight's dinner, a handful of onions and a dish of dried beans.

4. Dismantle the bathroom, shut off the water, remove the electric wiring.

5. Take away the house itself, and move the family into a toolshed.

6. Remove all the other houses in the neighborhood, and set up in this place a shantytown.

7. Cancel all subscriptions to newspapers, magazines and book clubs. This is no great loss, as our family is now illiterate.

8. Leave one small radio for the whole shantytown.

9. Move the nearest clinic or hospital ten miles away and put a midwife in charge instead of a doctor.

10. Throw out the bankbooks, stock certificates, pension plans and insurance policies, and leave the family a cash hoard of $5.

11. Give the head of the family three tenant acres to cultivate. On this he can raise $300 in cash crops, of which one-third will go to the landlord and one-tenth to the local moneylender.

12. Lop off twenty-five to thirty years in life expectancy. And so we have brought our typical American family down to the very bottom of the human scale.

IMPENDING CRISIS. *Poverty in India* by V. M. Dandekar and Nilakantha Rath (1971), is the title of an in-depth study that covers all aspects of the problem. Poverty in India is defined as a problem of low national income and its unequal distribution, of slow-paced development, and of inequitable distribution of the small gains of development.

For a nation confronted with a socioeconomic crisis of poverty as India is, resources simply cannot be counted on to provide basic institutions, amenities, and services for an additional 13.5 million people each year. If the basic services and amenities of India's new entries into its present population of 640 million (1979) are to be met each year, the annual requirements will be 2.5 million new houses, forty thousand additional teachers, and 4 million new jobs.

Since poverty is perpetuated by the inequitable distribution of the means of production resulting in an unjust distribution of national products at a time when the world's resources are shrinking, population growth greatly magnifies and intensifies the issue.

While reliable statistics on unemployment in the developing countries are hard to come by, it is generally accepted that as many as one-third of the rural people are either unemployed or partially employed. The ever-increasing plague of unemployment in these countries deprives people of purchasing power which is what causes hunger.

In examining the size of the labor force in the year 2000, we see that its expected growth will be between 1.6 and 1.9 percent per annum reaching 2,588 million by the year 2000. Over three-quarters of this labor force will be in the developing countries.

The projected labor figures for the last third of this century reveal that the unemployment burden will fall most heavily on the young. For example, by the year 2000 in India, 70.8 percent of the male population will be under twenty-nine years of age. Since at this youthful age ambitions and yearnings are the greatest, it takes little imagination to sense the yeast of political unrest fermenting.

POPULATION PRESSURES AND RESOURCES. Population pressures are already being felt in particular relationship to the four major resources—land, water, energy, and food.

Land. There is still room for more equitable land distribution through land tenure legislation, which places a ceiling on holdings and requires that the owner till the land. But the sobering truth is that the available cultural land will hardly make a dent in providing the landless laborers and small holders with economically viable units.

On a worldwide basis, only two areas—Africa and Latin America—have additional potentially productive land available for agriculture. While some wasteland and arid areas have the potential of being brought into production, costs are presently prohibitive.

Water. Water enough to meet human consumption and agricultural production has recently become a world concern. The United National Conference on Water, held March 14-25, 1977, in Argentina, was attended by 116 United Nations member states. As in all United Nations conferences, there were areas of disagreement; yet there was consensus on the central point—without an intense global effort to prevent it, the world faces a water crisis before the end of this century.

Three forces are at work that place an increasing demand on water: a doubling of the population early in the next century; rapidly diminishing natural resources; and rising standards of living, resulting in an even greater demand. Water demands are already exceeding supplies in many areas. United Nations' studies point out that adequate supplies of drinking water are not available for at least one-fifth of the world's city dwellers and three-fourths of the rural people.

Energy. Energy and mineral resources, vital to industry, modernized agriculture, and family living, grow more critical each day with the birth of 300,000 babies.

It is unrealistic to assume that the presently known resource base can sustain a doubling of the population with a continuous increase in per capita consumption of fuels, minerals, and food. Hard choices will have to be made. We cannot go on forever spending and consuming at higher levels. The time is at hand to acknowledge that the earth's bounty must be more equitably shared for both the present and future generations.

Food. Assuming the world's population will continue to expand at the present rate, it will double every thirty-five to forty years, and the anticipated food needs are staggering. Even if the world marketing system could distribute the global food available to everyone on an egalitarian basis, world food production would need to double over the next thirty-five years.

All doubts about food being a world problem should have been dispelled by two 1974 United Nations World Conferences: the World Population Conference held in Bucharest, Rumania, in August; and the World Food Conference held in Rome, Italy, in November. Largely because of droughts throughout the world in 1972 and 1974 and the sale by United States to Russia of the last of its grain reserves, the world's food reserves had been drawn down to about thirty-one days. When the Food and Agriculture Organization (FAO) took account of world population and agricultural production trends and projected world food needs to 1986, it came up with the startling revelation that developing countries would have a market demand deficit of 65 million tons.

Cognizant of the 1974 Rome Food Conference findings and of FAO's projected 1986 annual food deficit anticipated for developing countries, the Washington, D.C. based International Food Policy Research Institute has continued to keep abreast of agricultural production prospects throughout the developing countries of the world. The Institute's findings, as of April 1977, were reported by the Interim Director in a Conference on International Food Policy Issues:

> The developing market economies (DME) included in our study contain about 2.0 billion people, roughly half of all people on earth. By 1990, the U.N. medium population projection for these countries totals 2.0 billion people. While there are some demographers who believe that more progress than indicated by the U.N. projection will be made in containing population growth, it is unlikely within the time period considered that population will be significantly below the projected number.
>
> About 90 percent of these people will live in food-deficit countries, if past cereal production trends prevail. In 1975, gross deficits (the sum of individual country shortfalls) totaled some 36 million tons of cereals. By 1990, the shortfall in meeting demand from population and income growth at 1975 prices might well range from 120 to 145 million tons.
>
> Almost two-thirds of all people in DME countries will live in *low-income* food-deficit countries (countries with less than $300 GNP per capita in 1973). These are largely in Asia and Sub-Sahara Africa. Their food deficit, which was 12 million tons in 1975, is projected to rise to 70–85 million tons by 1990. This is the real core of the world food problem. Just to provide per capita consumption at the 1975 level will require some 35 million tons over and above the production trend projection. Most countries in this category have bleak prospects for earning enough foreign exchange to purchase commercially.

The oil countries of Indonesia and Nigeria may be exceptions, and perhaps also the Philippines. On the other hand, few can afford to reduce consumption, which for most of their population is already below standard. This emphasizes the need to improve production in these countries from the historical rate of 2.4 percent a year to about 4.0 percent, since the alternative of obtaining such massive quantities of food aid seems to be out of the question.

There is little likelihood that this projection will change within the next decade.

It seems clear that if developing countries provide leadership for agricultural development and generate needed resources to increase their purchases on world markets that the world's resources are capable of supporting the production of enough food to meet a doubling of the world's population.

It is one thing to visualize enough food being produced to meet a doubled population, and quite another to accept that millions of people are likely to face major food shortages because of the failure of the market system to move food from where it will be produced to where it will be needed. Finally, given the present and expected continuing low level of world food reserves and the projected population growth, weather will be a major factor in determining when, where, and how many people experience extreme food shortages, and perhaps even famine conditions.

NATIONAL AND GLOBAL IMPLICATIONS. In literature it is common to find food, population, poverty, water, minerals, and energy defined as global problems, and they are. But first, they must be accepted as national problems. Only as national political leaders face the realities and commit themselves and their nations' resources can these issues, which have global implications, be solved.

To understand the emerging explosive nature of poverty in a developing country such as India, for example, one must differentiate between the country today as a self-governing republic and the historical India with long cultural traditions. It certainly should be obvious that when people were governed by a foreign power, the poor had few alternatives. Foreign rulers were not primarily concerned about providing opportunities for their subjects to develop as human beings.

As self-governing, sovereign nations, the people living in poverty can see for themselves the disparity between their way of life and the life-style of those who control the production resources. The poor know that without access to production resources, their children and grandchildren will sink deeper into poverty as the elite get richer.

The world community in addressing world poverty, should understand that the most meaningful constraint the poor countries face in their efforts to eliminate hunger and confront poverty is poverty itself. And since the poor people of the world typically have limited access to birth control methods, future population increases will come primarily from the poor.

The population problem among the poor compounds itself just like interest. Knowing the chances for survival of their offspring are risky, these people purposefully have more children than they know they can afford to increase the possibility of survival of at least one male child and possibly more. With no dependable social security measures in the majority of developing countries, the one best hope is to produce surviving offspring whom culture dictates shall support their parents in old age.

While recent studies show that population growth rates in the developing world are beginning to decline slightly, an alarming statistic has come to light. A partial explanation for the declining growth rate is an *increase in the death rate in some areas.* It is undoubtedly true that where increasing death rates are occurring, lack of food and poor nutrition are major contributing factors.

Governments in their frustration have in some instances resorted to draconian measures, the likes of which were known only in science fiction a few years ago. The population problem will be solved one way or another—either by rational and humanitarian means or irrationally and inhumanely.

REFERENCES

Dandekar, V. M., and Rath, Nilakantha. *Poverty in India.* Bombay: Krishna Raj, 1971.

Edwards, Edgar O., ed. *Employment in Developing Nations.* New York: Columbia Univ. Press, 1974.

Osborn, Fairfield. *Our Crowded Planet: Essays on the Pressures of Population.* Garden City, N.Y.: Doubleday, 1962.

Pohlman, Edward, ed. *Population: A Clash of Prophets.* New York: New American Library, 1973.

Since Bucharest—and the Future. International Population Conference of the World Population Society. Washington, D.C.: World Population Society, 1976.

World Population Growth and Response. 1965–1975 A Decade of Global Action. Washington, D.C.: Population Reference Bureau, Apr. 1976.

3

DEVELOPMENT CAPITAL

No issue has been more worrisome to the governments of developing countries than that of financing their development. Most developing countries came into being about as naked financially as a newborn baby. Imperial rule had impoverished the colonial village. Unlike the newborn child who had parents to finance his growth from infancy to early adulthood, governments of the new nations that emerged following World War II were confronted with more problems and needed more funds than the governments possessed or could generate.

POLICIES: INVOLVEMENT AND SUPPORT. Looking back to the early development commitments of the new inexperienced governments, one can see that scarce government finances were dissipated in providing services to the people without involving them in the development of an economic base essential to the support of new services.

This early attempt of new governments to do things for the people had two negative effects. Many of the services, while essential, were imposed on the people rather than allowing them to participate in the decisions that they wanted and needed the services. Furthermore, the government took the initiative to finance the services without requiring that people contribute to the cost. Thus people have grown to expect governments to continue funding projects and programs.

The basic financial consideration confronting governments of developing countries is how to generate enough capital to invest in projects that will provide, with time, all people with visible evidence that they can earn and ascend the ladder toward a more satisfying and secure way of life. A government that looks to its people to participate in improving their own level of living will find that when its limited finances serve as a support resource for people's involvement and funds, sustained progress can come from limited government development capital.

While a few of the problems confronting the world's poor can be solved through individual initiative and effort, most of the people's problems can only be resolved through group effort. Governments do not have enough money to solve all the complex social problems through government directed and financed projects. While many rural development projects require direct government expenditure, whenever feasible, government funds should be channeled through people's organizations and institutions.

Funds required to help the people achieve a better and more secure level of living greatly exceed both present and potential available monies. When projects have the potential of becoming economically feasible, government funds should be made available in the form of repayable loans. The people will have a greater stake in the projects' success when institutions and organizations sign for loans on behalf of all. In addition, the repaid loan funds can be used to finance additional development.

There is a development principle here. Governments of developing countries should adopt a philosophy which says, "It is what they do with what they have that counts." Governments have untapped and underdeveloped human resources. Moreover, they are confronted with scarce capital for development. As human resources are developed, the people themselves will become the driving force of change.

While accepting that both the rate and quality of development will be directly related to the development of human resources, caution must be practiced in putting a disproportionate amount of scarce development capital into social overhead expenditures. At least the minimum needs of people must be met through educational and health services and institutions. Also, funds must be available for institutions to serve small-farm agriculture and economic enterprises including village industries.

Furthermore, great care should be exercised in putting scarce development capital into physical infrastructures. When roads and transport systems can be shown to contribute to the development of the economic base, they should be funded.

Illustrations abound throughout the world supporting the conclusion that when the priority of development projects reflects the people's felt needs, they will contribute some of their limited funds and join in a group effort for the benefit of all. People should be educated and stimulated to look to themselves when solving problems rather than to government. But governments need to prove they are trustworthy and socially concerned resources.

If people are to save and invest their earnings in development projects that will benefit them, people's banks, convenient to the rural areas, must be established. While it will take time for people to entrust their savings to banks, there is ample evidence that people can be counted on to make regular deposits and honor payments on due loans. Limited capital can go a long way in generating new capital for development and providing the people with a sense of achievement, if the project chosen has the potential of becoming economically successful.

ECONOMIC GROWTH VS INTEGRATED RURAL DEVELOPMENT. Accepting that capital for development will continue to be in short supply, development objectives will determine capital requirements as well as sources from which funds will have to be mobilized.

When development emphasis is on economic growth and the strategy chosen is on capital-intensive projects, the mobilization of out-of-country capital becomes a necessity. If, however, the development emphasis is to improve the quality of life for everyone and the development strategy is integrated rural development, the bulk of development capital can be mobilized from within the country under a policy of careful phasing and balancing of social services and growth-generating projects. Admitting that the bulk of capital funds for integrated rural development can be mobilized from within the countries in no way implies that integrated rural development will be cheap, or that it will not require outside capital. It will. Development capital for integrated rural development, having as its objective the improvement of the level of living of all people, will be essential in supplementing programs whose cost exceeds the people's resources.

How development funds are made available for integrated rural development will greatly influence the amount of development funds expended. Government funds should be known to be available and released under agreed conditions. The people should contribute their full share. They should give a clear signal that their participation is assured in carrying the projects forward and to completion. Most important will be the people's understanding of how the projects and programs contribute to their own advancement in achieving a more secure way of life.

GUIDELINES: CAPITAL-INTENSIVE PROJECTS. It would be a grave mistake to assume that just because the emphasis is on programs

to improve levels of living through rural development and on the involvement of people in generating new capital there will not be a need for capital-intensive projects. What will be important will be policy guidelines in selecting capital-intensive projects that will advance the national policy to improve the level of living of all. Industries should be selected on the basis of manufactured products essential to development and on the consumer needs of most people. Poor countries cannot afford to waste scarce resources on luxury-producing industries.

When irrigation projects are selected for capital-intensive investments, they should be backed by policies which assure that the benefits will go to farmers on an equitable basis. Funds spent on transportation and infrastructures should be designed to relieve inequities within countries and contribute to a balanced national growth.

In the past thirty years, governments of the developing countries have accepted foreign economic aid and all too frequently approved foreign investments on projects that donors chose to fund. For the governments of the developing countries to succeed, they—not the foreign donors nor the foreign investors—must decide to accept foreign aid and investments only when they can be shown to contribute to the developing countries' own clearly stated national objectives for improving the level of living of everyone.

The world community is far from agreement as to the initial amount of capital developing countries will require and the period of time needed to alleviate the conditions that cause poverty. But one can be certain that developing countries cannot do the job without having access to foreign capital over a very long period of time.

Developing countries need foreign capital, but all would be wise to keep their commitments and plans for development balanced against a realistic projection of resources they can generate. Foreign development capital should always be supportive of, but not central to, the countries' achieving a higher quality of life for all the people.

Yet it is imperative that industrialized nations stop viewing the developing countries as relief clients. Furthermore, foreign investors should accept that the larger percentage of development resources needed by developing countries be channeled from governments to governments.

As the industrialized nations come to understand their increasing dependence on the world markets for minerals and oil, they can be expected to see that it will be in their economic, social, and political interest to be supportive of the developing countries' need for a reliable source of development capital.

REFERENCES

Behrman, Jack N. "Toward a New International Economic Order." Paper presented at Atlantic Institute for International Affairs. Paris, Oct. 1974.

Fergusun, C. Clyde Jr. Statement of United States Delegation to the 31st session of ECOSOC. New Delhi, Feb. 28, 1975.

Gardner, Richard N. "The Hard Road to World Order." *Foreign Affairs,* Apr. 1974, p. 556.

Howe, James W., et al. "The United States and Developing World." Agenda for Action, 1974. Overseas Development Council.

Nyerere, Julius K. Address at Howard University, Washington, D.C., Aug. 5, 1977.

Schmidt, Helmut. "The Struggle for the World Product," *Foreign Affairs,* Apr. 1974, p. 451.

Sewell, John, et al. "The United States and World Department." Agenda 1977. Overseas Department Council.

Stewart, Maxwell S. *Food for the World's Hungry.* Public Affairs Pamphlet no. 511, 1974.

Williams, Maurice J. *Development Corporation: Efforts and Policies of the Members of the Development Assistance Committee, 1977 Review.* Report for the Organization for Economic Cooperation and Development. Paris: Nov. 1977.

4

THE FREE MARKET SYSTEM

Economic theory tells us that prices are set by an agreement between seller and buyer; this has been the dominant philosophy behind the free market system. In practice things are not so simple. The manufacturers of machinery, for instance, have not compromised with the buyers of their goods. In our current international system the developed nations are the ones who have been associated with production of manufactured goods. The buyers of these goods are the developing nations, who have no choice since they cannot manufacture these goods.

That there must be greater sharing on the part of the rich industrialized nations with the poor developing countries should not be a major world issue for long. The debate should focus on the strategies as well as the dimensions of the assistance now needed. Concern is also growing over developing countries' weak and inadequate commitments to carry out internal social and economic reforms.

GOALS FOR A NEW INTERNATIONAL WORLD ORDER. The call for a new economic order, initiated by the developing countries, was directed toward the industrialized nations. Increasingly, this call for sharing the world's production resources is referred to as the case of the poor southern developing countries appealing to the rich northern industrialized nations for a greater share of the world's production resources.

The debate on the new world order must conform to the idea that if it is to bring about the proper response from the rich industrialized nations, the new world order must start within the poor developing countries. The gap between the "haves" and the "have nots" is probably far more dramatic within the developing countries than it is between the developing countries and the industrialized nations. If the poor are to gain access to production resources within the developing countries, revolutionary reform—not mere change—will have to be accepted as a viable alternative.

In 1974, the need for a "new international economic order" (NIEO) became the dominant topic for many international forums. Suddenly, the focus was on North/South problems. The first meeting in Geneva in 1964 of seventy-seven developing countries at the United Nations Conference on Trade and Development had concentrated on the same problems for a decade. Perhaps in 1974, after the oil embargo, the world began to visualize the implications of "future scarcities" and the need for their consideration on an international level.

Since 1974 there have been numerous international forums. The "Lima Declaration" in March 1975 set forth the goal of increasing developing nations' world industries production from 8 percent to 20 percent by the year 2000. In February 1976 the "Group of 77" developing countries drew up the "Manila Declaration" which put forward seventeen economic reforms. In addition to the commodity-related issues mentioned above, the developing nations wanted to renegotiate their increasing external debt obligations, have greater access to existing technology, increase resource-transference mechanisms, and most importantly, have fuller participation in decision-making procedures in the existing international system. In short, they wanted a greater voice in world trade and finances. The developing countries were asking for a fair share in a system that was established when most of these nations were colonies.

Having raised the issue of equality of opportunity within the world forum of the United Nations, the developing countries can be expected to intensify pressures on the developed countries for more of a partnership relation. Above all, the developing countries want to be free from what appears to them to be a welfare role in which they are the clients.

AREAS AND STRATEGIES FOR REFORM

World Trade. The atmosphere in the developing countries has undergone dramatic change in emphasis. Today the emphasis is on trade, not aid, as had been the situation for the past two decades. These emerging nations produce mostly nonfuel primary commodities, the main ones being cocoa, coffee, copper, sugar, cotton, jute, rubber, sisal, tea, tin, bananas, bauxite, beef and veal, iron ore, rice, and wool. The interest of the poor nations is in uplifting production, marketing, and distribution, as well as in stabilizing prices and export earnings from these goods. Roughly 60 percent of

TABLE 4.1. Flow of Official Development Assistance from Development Assistance Committee Members Measured as a Percentage of Gross National Product[a]

	1965	1970	1975	1976	1977	1978	1979	1980	1981	1982	1983	1984	198
Australia	.53	.59	.60	.42	.45	.45	.45	.46	.47	.47	.48	.49	.5(
Austria	.11	.07	.17	.12	.24	.27	.28	.29	.29	.30	.30	.31	.3(
Belgium	.60	.46	.59	.51	.46	.55	.54	.58	.60	.62	.65	.67	.7(
Canada	.19	.42	.55	.46	.50	.52	.46	.47	.47	.48	.50	.50	.5(
Denmark	.13	.38	.58	.56	.60	.75	.69	.70	.70	.71	.71	.72	.7(
Finland[b]	.02	.07	.18	.18	.17	.18	.20	.21	.21	.22	.23	.24	.2(
France	.76	.66	.62	.62	.60	.57	.57	.57	.58	.58	.59	.60	.6(
Germany	.40	.32	.40	.31	.27	.31	.32	.33	.33	.34	.34	.35	.3(
Italy	.10	.16	.11	.13	.10	.06	.10	.10	.09	.13	.11	.10	.1(
Japan	.27	.23	.23	.20	.21	.23	.25	.26	.26	.27	.28	.28	.2(
Netherlands	.36	.61	.75	.82	.85	.82	.90	.93	.93	.93	.94	.95	.9(
New Zealand[c]		.23	.52	.41	.39	.34	.30	.27	.27	.27	.29	.31	.3(
Norway	.16	.32	.66	.70	.83	.90	.92	.94	.96	.97	.98	.99	1.0(
Sweden	.19	.38	.82	.82	.99	.90	.93	.94	.95	.96	.98	.98	1.0(
Switzerland	.09	.15	.19	.19	.19	.20	.21	.21	.22	.23	.23	.24	.2(
United Kingdom	.47	.36	.37	.38	.37	.40	.39	.40	.40	.40	.40	.41	.4(
United States[d]	.49	.31	.26	.25	.22	.23	.22	.22	.22	.22	.22	.22	.2(

SOURCE: Address to the Board of Governors by Robert S. McNamara, president; World Bank. Belgrade, Yugoslavia, Oct. 2, 1979. World Bank publication.
[a]Historical figures through 1977 and preliminary estimates for 1978 are from OECD. Those for 1979–85 are based on OECD and World Bank estimates of growth of GNP, on information on budget appropriations for aid, and on aid policy statements by governments. They are projections, not predictions, of what will occur unless action not now planned takes place.
[b]Finland became a member of DAC in January 1975.
[c]New Zealand became a member of DAC in 1973, ODA figures for New Zealand are not available for 1965.
[d]In 1949, at the beginning of the Marshall Plan, U.S. Official Development Assistance amounted to 2.79% of GNP.

the foreign exchange of the developing countries is derived from the sale of these commodities. Other sources of foreign exchange are manufactured goods, minerals, and services. These commodities comprise about 75 percent of the nonfuel commodity trade in the developing countries.

It is not that the industrialized developed nations have failed to provide assistance to the developing countries during the past thirty years. They have helped. But the quantum of aid has not been in relation to the developing countries' needs or the capabilities of the developed countries to assist. Table 4.1 presents a picture of development assistance based on the Gross National Product (GNP) of developed countries from 1965 through a projection of assistance through 1985.

Whereas humanitarianism has been the basis for aid to developing countries since World War II, now self-interest, politically and economically, can often be the motivation for increased aid. The United States, with about 6 percent of the world's population, will be using more than 42 percent of the world's minerals in the eighties. The United States looked to agricultural exports, which were $24 billion in 1977, to cover a portion of the $45 billion oil imports bill in 1977.

Since costs for oil imports are rising faster than sales of agricultural exports, a case can be made that it would be in the United States' interest to assist in the development of the economies of the developing countries so they can buy United States food grain on the world market.

Tariffs. From the above discussion one would expect that if poor nations processed their own primary goods, they would at least be able to set high prices in the same manner as the industrial nations do. However, their goods meet barriers that keep them away from the "free market." The tariff rates increase on a product as the degree of processing increases. Clothing, noncotton textiles, and shoes are good examples of commodities that are often stalled by these barriers. Nontariff barriers that the developed nations impose on goods from the developing world also exist. These include standards of performance or safety, customs, and administrative regulations or procedures.

Shipping Rates. Even if trade barriers were lifted, goods from the poor nations would still be expensive because of the present structure of shipping rates. It is much cheaper to ship raw materials from developing to industrialized nations than to ship manufactured goods from developing nations.

The injustice in the present structure of fixing shipping rates has been pointed out by President Nyerere of Tanzania:

Freight rates are mostly fixed by shipper's cartel—OPEC did not invent the idea of combining to fix the price of a vital commodity! This cartel has an apparently ineradicable bias against carrying processed goods away from East Africa: for a ton, it would cost $41 to ship raw sisal and $73 to ship twine from and to the same port, with similar differentials between cotton lint and textiles, hides and leathers, and so on.

Commodity Prices. Fluctuations in the price of commodities is a constant concern of the developing nations. While the price of manufactured goods from the industrial nations is always going up, the costs of primary goods move up and down, mostly down. If they do move up, they do not stay there long. For example, between 1972 and 1975, the price of copper fell 60 percent, while sugar fell 81 percent. The price of coffee recently rose very high, but has already come down. The fluctuations in price result in fluctuations in total earnings from year to year, making planned economic strategy a complex issue for many developing nations.

The slow growth of raw materials for export is sometimes a result of strong competition from synthetic materials. On top of these hurdles the poor nations have to face natural problems. Adverse weather conditions and crop disease are factors that must be considered and dealt with by the farm producers in the developing countries.

Finance. The developed nations enjoy special treatment in the international financial system. Superimposed on the already grim situation of the poor nations is the inequitable distribution of the Special Drawings Rights (SDR) in the International Monetary Fund. It has been estimated that the Third World, containing over 70 percent of the world's population, received less than 4 percent of the $126 billion of international liquidity created during the last two decades. And up to the end of 1974, 74.7 percent of the SDR created have been allocated to the rich countries and 25.3 percent to the poor ones. The poor nations would like to see an alternative allocation system based on proportional fund quotas. This present system promotes trade between the nations, stripping purchasing power from the poor nations. Jack N. Behrman in a section on "Energy, Inflation and International Economic Relations" in his study entitled *Toward a New International Economic Order* has emphasized: "Like the market, the monetary system is only a mechanism, for money has no value of its own (apart from commodity money)."

Technology Transfer. The United Nations Conference on Trade and Development is considering proposals that will improve the overall terms of technology transfer. These recommendations will address the following problems:

1. The lopsided bargaining power of buyers and sellers of technology and the unfair pricing structure that comes about in a monopolistic market that is biased toward the technology sellers.

2. The inappropriateness of transferred technology in terms of materials, capital, and personnel for the poor nations.

3. The patent system, which has most often prompted profit-making ventures.

4. The frequency of "package deal" agreements that hinder the optimum use of the poor nations' resources. These, together with restrictive contractual clauses, give greater power to technology sellers to determine the type of operation—whether capital-intensive or labor-intensive.

Resource Scarcities. The world will never forget the 1973 oil embargo imposed by the OPEC countries. These countries used the same familiar tactic of industrialized nations and raised the price of oil.

Their price hike had far-reaching implications for the world's economy. The developed nations complained about the OPEC action, and so did the poor nations. However, one should not get the impression that they both suffered equally. Actually, this action hurt the developing nations more than the developed nations. It could be argued that the developing nations have been partial beneficiaries, because the petrodollars have been invested in their countries. Yet for the developing nations OPEC's action is having a twofold effect. At the very time when the developing countries were accepting the importance of fertilizer and other agricultural inputs derived from oil, the sharp increase in the price of oil has pushed the price of fertilizer out of the reach of small farmers with limited resources. For the developing countries that have moved away from animal power for agriculture toward tractor power and diesel pumps for irrigation, the high cost and the drain on scarce foreign exchange for oil imports is having an adverse effect on agricultural production.

The second effect has been an increase in debts. While the debts of the developing countries are increasing from 20 to 25 percent a year, the biggest borrowers are the oil-rich and high potential oil-rich countries like Mexico, Indonesia, Nigeria, and Nicaragua. Some borrow for straight oil production, like Mexico, Peru, and Argentina. Others, like Venezuela, borrow for industry and public works.

The rapidly growing countries, such as South Korea, are also heavy borrowers. The poorest of the poor developing countries like Ghana, Sierra Leone, Liberia, and Senegal are moving away from borrowing and going toward grants-in-aid. In 1971, the debt of developing nations was $80 billion, or double the 1965 figure. The yearly burden of paying the principal and interest on this debt in 1972 was about $7.3 billion, equivalent to 11 percent of the exports of the poor nations that year. In 1973, this figure stood at $89.2 billion; by 1978 it had jumped to $315 billion. As a consequence, the developing nations have been forced to cut back on imports essential for economic progress. They have had to use their hard earned foreign exchange and borrow from private and international banks.

The situation is alarming. The debt services payments could outstrip exports profits from many of the developing nations. If the situation is not arrested, there could be a reverse resource channeling from the poor nations to the rich ones of compound interest on the debts. The neediest nations are being forced to resort to private lending sources offering harder terms. While not yet a trend, there is growing evidence of an increase in the flow of resources to the developing countries.

   A global political orientation is needed to direct itself to the problem of resource scarcity. The problem will be not only one of increasing total supplies of scarce raw materials, but also of ensuring a fair share to the world community. The current struggle over oil prices could be followed by similar struggles over the prices of other important raw materials. If the situation is not remedied, one could imagine the emergence of a "copper cartel," "chrome cartel," or "phosphate cartel."

GNP View of Development. The Gross National Product view of development is closely linked to the problem of economic order, internationally and within nations. For many years, exports have been focusing on the GNP as a measure of progress. This view unfortunately has two shortcomings. First, it disregards the question of distribution. The developing countries have lacked a process for transferring profits from increased GNP to the lower income groups. Instead, they hope that prosperity will "trickle down" to the poor. Ironically, rich countries find it necessary to plan for production but are hesitant to plan for distribution. The second weakness of the GNP view of development is its inclusion of all economic activity in its computation. It covers all increases in production, whether of luxury goods or basic necessities. The GNP does not reveal the quality of life, types of jobs, or skills that are available in a particular environment. Thus it is possible to increase GNP while failing to meet essential human needs. The production of a B-52, MIG-24, or neutron bomb will be associated with a rise in GNP, but it remains to be seen what a hungry man can do with these items.

INTERDEPENDENCE. The bonds of interdependence have been steadily growing. This view was emphasized by Cyrus Vance, secretary of state, on February 27, 1978, when he addressed the National Governors' Association:

. . . We have far too much at stake to benefit, in any sense, from a new wave of international protectionism. One out of every eight manufacturing jobs in the United States depends on exports. For every one of those jobs, another one—in a supporting industry—is created.
. . . Today, one out of every three dollars of U.S. corporate profits is derived from international activities.

   On another occasion, when addressing the national convention of the League of Women Voters on May 1, 1978, Secretary Vance commented: "Our economic health and our security are more closely tied today than ever before to the economic well-being and security of the developing world. Progress therefore means more jobs and more prosperity for the United States."

In addition to this refreshing rejoinder by Secretary Vance, there is further supporting evidence derived from trade information about the effect of interdependence and its economic benefits:

1. The nonoil-producing countries are a major market for American goods, taking one-quarter of the total exports last year, or about the same share of total exports that goes to Europe and the Communist countries combined.

2. Products from less developed countries including raw materials such as tin, copper, bauxite, and lead accounted for nearly one-quarter of the total American imports last year.

3. The United States gained more than $7 billion from direct price investment in the developing world in 1975. And in 1976, developing countries absorbed nearly $11 billion from direct foreign investment.

4. In the export of agricultural products in 1977, developing countries purchased one-half of the exports of cotton, 65 percent of wheat, and nearly 70 percent of rice.

5. The American economy benefits substantially as aid dollars are spent in the United States to buy commodities and services. For example, for every dollar paid by America into the World Bank and the regional development banks for Latin America, Asia, and Africa, about two dollars has been spent in the United States economy.

In the past, the rich nations have avoided the issue of unfairness in trade patterns by simply saying that the market is at fault. But it should be quite evident that the market by itself is not the problem. The market is no more than a mechanism. It has no power to control or to decide, and it only meters what goes in and out of it.

Heretofore, much attention has been paid to mechanical and technical answers, leaving the system alone. The heart of the matter is that the free market system is unjust and should be overhauled so that economic justice may prevail.

The marketing system should be conceived for men, and not men for the system. Needed are new rules so that profits flow two ways rather than one way. The "gap" must be narrowed instead of widened, and an elevated involvement of all nations, rather than domination by a few developed nations, must be expected.

In pressing for a "new economic order," the developing countries have raised the right questions: Will rapid economic growth eventually produce equality? and, Is it tolerable, in the meantime, to allow a generation or two to die?

REFERENCES

Behrman, Jack N. "Toward a New International Economic Order." Paper presented at Atlantic Institute for International Affairs. Paris: Oct. 1974.

Fergusun, C. Clyde Jr. Statement of United States Delegation to the 31st session of ECOSOC. New Delhi: Feb. 28, 1975.

Gardner, Richard N. "The Hard Road to World Order," *Foreign Affairs,* Apr. 1974, p. 556.

Howe, James W., et al. "The United States and Developing World." Agenda for Action, 1974. Overseas Development Council.

Nyerere, Julius K. Address at Howard University, Washington, D.C., Aug. 5, 1977.

Sewell, John, et al. "The United States and World Department." Agenda 1977. Overseas Department Council.

5

NUTRITION FOR SURVIVAL

Chancellor Willy Brandt, addressing the United Nations General Assembly in 1973, made the telling point that "Morally it makes no difference whether a man is killed in war or is condemned to starve to death by the indifference of others." Fortunately, increased sensitivity to the plight of the hungry has been reflected in development strategies. Consequently, the seventies will be known as the decade when the developing countries began changing their policies and strategies from economic growth measured by the GNP to quality of life measured by the achievement of a nutritionally adequate diet for all people.

This new emphasis in development policies and strategies is evidence of a fundamental change in values. Economic growth is a materialistic value, and quality of life is a humanistic value. Quality of life, in this context, takes on as much specificity as does economic growth.

When developing countries' policies are directed toward improving the quality of life for all, one definite objective should be a minimally nutritious diet for everyone. This diet should be based on the energy intake (specific caloric requirements) essential for the average healthy person.

The Washington, D.C. based International Food Policy Research Institute report of July 1977 stated that some 1.2 to 1.5 billion people in countries with developing market economies were characterized as undernourished in 1975. This equals two-thirds of all the people in these countries.

Because the energy (calorie) requirements of individuals depend on four variables interrelated in a complex way (physical activity, body size and composition, age, and climate and other ecological considerations), it is meaningless to define a minimally nutritional diet on a global basis. The nutritionist in each country will have to research the calorie requirements for various categories of the population who are expected to perform tasks related to earning and living in good health.

FOUR SUPPORTING POLICIES. To achieve the national objective that all people receive a minimally nutritional diet will require acceptance and implementation of the following four supporting policies: to provide all able-bodied people an opportunity to earn enough to pay for food required for an essential diet; to diversify agriculture and perfect the marketing and distribution system so the required food will be produced and made available on the markets; to improve the nutritional quality of the diet by fortifying processed grains with vitamins; and to educate and provide a diversified balanced diet for pregnant women and school-age children.

Because of the low state of the economies of the developing countries, even with the needed political commitments and political will, it will take time and careful husbandry of scarce finances to provide the opportunities for the millions who are either partially employed or unemployed to work, earn, and achieve.

No government should continue to be indifferent to the plight of the poor, living in squalor with barely enough food to survive. However, it is important to understand that it would financially bankrupt the developing countries to implement immediately policies to provide, through government, the requisite quantity and quality of additional food for the poor to have a minimally nutritional diet. Eventually, policies and political commitments must be made if we are to see the day when all people will be assured the diet they need.

The process of changing values related to eating habits will require sustained education and diversified agricultural crops in areas where soil, water, and climate are favorable. Where diversification is not feasible, markets will have provide the supporting and supplementary items for the minimum nutritional diet.

Policies related to shifting from single food-crop to multiple-cropping and diversified agriculture must be implemented. The most crucial change in this process will be from farming to meet subsistence needs to farm production aimed at both quantity and variety in agricultural goods to sell on the market where feasible. The governments' pricing policies cannot by themselves provide the total motivation for farmers to diversify food crop, but diversification is not likely to take place without reliable markets and trustworthy pricing policies.

Another set of values related to providing the conditions for producing essential crops to meet the needed energy requirements are survival values tied in with a sense of security in continuing to farm as they have for generations. Until those in poverty can feel secure, they will not risk their chances of survival.

We can readily see that moving a population group from looking upon food to survive to placing a value on food to meet calorie requirements of a nutritional diet is complex and must be approached on a number of fronts. We should also understand that the changes in values related to eating habits, along with the agricultural production changes and reforms required for people to be productively employed, will take time.

Policy 1—Economic Enterprise. For governments to deliver on policies of assuring the people that food requirements for a minimally essential diet will be available year after year, national policies will have to emphasize education, diversified agriculture, reduction of losses, and storage in good years to stabilize the lean years. But these and other related policies will not by themselves make it possible for everyone to have a minimally nutritional diet, unless all people have a chance to work and earn enough to meet their basic needs.

Policy 2—Marketing and Distribution. In a comprehensive set of national policies dealing with adequate nutrition, both industrial development and export policies will need to be reexamined.

If the new emphasis and policies are to improve the level of living of all the people, industrial development policies must change from using scarce foreign exchange, supporting industries producing goods for the small, affluent elite class, to supporting agricultural development oriented toward meeting the nutritional needs of everyone. To provide employment opportunities for more people to earn enough to pay for a nutritious family diet will require supporting and development of economic enterprises in rural areas and dispersal of small industries producing goods needed by all the people, especially the poor.

Governments committed to providing the conditions for all to have enough food to meet the essentials of good physical and mental health must urgently reexamine their policies of using scarce agricultural land to grow crops for export. The first call for productive agricultural land must be to meet the conditions so that all people may have a nutritious diet.

A minimally adequate diet that provides energy becomes the fuel that stokes the engine in making labor productive in the policy shift from capital-intensive projects to labor-intensive ones. Unless labor can become more productive, intensification of labor means intensification of drudgery—not a rewarding prospect.

Policy 3—Fortifying Foods. For the past thirty years, the developing countries have attempted, with little success, to take scientific medicine to the rural poor as a way to improve the people's health. The delivery cost of scientific medicine to the rural poor is prohibitive and as a result, only a few are reached. In the future, an adequately nutritional diet should be looked upon as one way to prevent ill health and provide the basis for "being in good health."

The milling industries that process food grains into edible form can, through vitamin enrichment, help assure that the food consumed meets both energy and calorie requirements. Nutrition researchers will have to solicit the support of the milling industries to add the recommended vitamins when milling food grains. Good nutrition holds the key to the physical and mental well-being of people and their capacity to lead and be actively included in the process of nation building.

The present food-deficit countries must be assisted through food-aid programs just to maintain life. The three major food-exporting countries—Canada, Australia, and the United States—can do little more through food-aid programs than contribute the difference between mere existence and slow but sure death from extreme malnutrition.

Policy 4—Family Nutrition. Community- and school-feeding programs for children and pregnant mothers over the past thirty years provide ample evidence that as families see the positive ways a well-balanced diet contributes to healthy bodies, there is increasing understanding about the meaning and importance of nutrition.

Malnutrition adversely affects both physical and mental development and interferes with children's capacity to concentrate and learn. It is therefore difficult to see how a country committed to improving the level of living for its people can achieve this objective without having policies, commitments, and programs to improve the nutritional quality of the diet for everyone.

WORLD SYSTEMS FOOD APPROACH. It will be difficult to reverse the world trend toward an increase in the percentage of the world's population who live in poverty and continuous fear of hunger. The challenge lies in the public rejection of world poverty and hunger as inevitable, and in worldwide support of an international systems approach to agriculture and rural development.

No country, regardless of whether it is presently a food exporter or chronic importer of food, should expect to meet its food, minerals, and energy needs in the future in traditional ways. The major food-exporting countries will become more vulnerable to the political forces of the mineral- and energy-producing countries as the minerals and oil become scarcer and more costly. Political instability, tensions, uprisings, and revolutions are almost certain to be the order of the day if the food–deficit developing countries are unable to meet their food deficits from world markets.

When the developing countries face crisis after crisis in meeting their food needs, as they most certainly will, the food-exporting countries will be confronted with hard choices in deciding which countries will be given first call on marketable food reserves.

Since the present marketing arrangements and the projected food-for-peace programs will not be able to meet the food deficits of the magnitude now projected for the developing countries, the world community can expect mounting international tensions and strong expressions of fierce nationalism. This can either lead to war, or, it is hoped, countries will see the wisdom of joining in a world food system approach.

One has only to reflect on the process of social change to understand that great changes result from major crises. Before many of the developing countries will commit themselves to a world food system approach, it is entirely conceivable they will do so only after they have experienced a famine in which millions of people die of starvation.

International cooperation, planning, and implementation of a world food system is likely to come out of necessity rather than humanitarianism. International cooperation in implementing a world food system will have to have something in it for all participating countries, and that something will have to contribute to each participating country's economic growth and political stability. It will have to assure food enough to meet the nutritional needs of all the people.

A world food system can provide, if its formulation is based on in-depth participation of the political power structure of each country, assignment of the resources from each country necessary for development and the guarantee that each country's food needs will be assured from the functioning of the system.

Within a world food system each country will have to shift from national policies and programs for food self-sufficiency to world policies that fully and effectively utilize each country's resources to maximize production within a world system. If the world community accepts the need for a world food system, there are at least three conditions that will have to be met if all people are to be assured an adequate nutritional diet:

The reduction of population must be accepted as a world priority in order to achieve a world free of hunger.

Developing countries must give high priority to the development of small-farm food-crop agriculture and implement land and institutional reforms.

The developed countries must accept the necessity of providing developing countries with the requisite resources for a food-producing rural economy.

It is one thing to understand and accept that the world's resources have the potential to produce enough food to meet the nutritional needs of a doubling world population; but it is quite another matter to understand there are upper limits on the world's resources, meeting an unchecked population growth. No one presently can predict at what point the world's resources will not be adequate for the task of feeding the world's population.

If worldwide population and family planning changes are as dramatic and consistent the next three decades as they have been the past two decades, then there is reason for optimism that the world's population could level off at between 8 and 10 billion by the middle of the next century. Unless population growth is checked, the most a world food system can be expected to achieve is to assure some equity in the distribution of food and prolong the period when there will not be enough food to meet minimum nutritional needs.

Whether or not there is a world food system in operation, there should be no misunderstanding about the commitment of developing countries to accelerate the rate of agricultural growth, especially for the small-farm food-crop sector. Even the most perfectly conceived world food system will falter, if not fail, when large segments of the population face food shortages that the governments cannot supplement, unless there is a political awakening and recognition that the present efforts and policies will lead to internal crisis.

It should be clear that developing countries must intensify their programs to earn foreign exchange, given the projection of an accelerating food deficit as the world's population continues to grow. The opening of markets within industrialized nations to developing countries, to sell their products and increase their foreign exchange earnings for food purchases on the world markets, will be a significant contribution in channeling food to the people who need it.

Over the past thirty years, the developed countries have generally taken a humanistic approach toward meeting the food needs of the developing countries. In the future, in addition to the humanistic approach, there must be an awareness of the economic and political advantages of assisting countries to strengthen their economies. Only as the developing countries grow in economic strength will they have the capacity to pay world market prices for food to meet their food deficit and develop stable political systems. As the developed countries understand that building up the economies of the developing countries will strengthen their own economies, one can be optimistic about the long-term future of international economic cooperation.

Since it will take time for the developing countries to implement a viable food-producing agriculture and gain acceptance of a world food system that will increase production rapidly enough to meet their growing food deficits, continuation of the United States' food-for-peace program will be essential. Millions of people from the developing countries who lack resources to purchase from the markets will face death from malnutrition and starvation without a substantial United States food program. Providing aid to prevent starvation is important, but food alone does not alleviate human misery.

A world security food reserve must be backed by policies that will contribute to the stability of prices for both producers and consumers. A world food reserve will contribute to political stability because the food needs of individual countries can be met without regard to political considerations.

When one finally understands the magnitude of the task of checking world population growth, of developing a modernized, small-farm agricultural production, of carrying out revolutionary governmental land and institutional reforms, and of accepting a world food system with world agricultural policies, one is compelled to accept a long time frame.

Being optimistic about the prospects of a world community in which the people can live free of hunger does not imply it will be achieved easily. Realistically, the policy of freedom from hunger for all will emerge from crises on how food, minerals, energy, and water are used and shared for the betterment of all people in both the developed and developing countries.

If we are to achieve a world where people can live free from the fear of hunger, we must cease speaking of developed and developing countries. We should work for policies and commitments acceptable to political leaders that will assure people in all countries an equal opportunity to basic human needs. We should insist that basic human needs universally mean gainful employment, a nutritious diet, education, clothing, shelter, health care, and a life of security and self-respect.

The world community will make a giant step forward in a long and turbulent journey when the United States implements as its foreign policy the words uttered by Secretary of State Cyrus Vance at the 1977 North/South Conference: "There should be a new economic system. In that system there must be equity; there must be growth; but, above all, there must be justice. We are prepared to build that new system."

REFERENCES

"The Arusha Declaration and TANU's Policy on Socialism and Self-Reliance." Dar es Salaam, Tanzania: Publicity Section of TANU, 1967.

Berg, Alan. *The Nutrition Factor.* Washington, D.C.: Brookings Institution, 1973.

Cleveland, Harlan, and Wilson, Thomas W., Jr. *Human Growth: An Essay on Growth, Values, and the Quality of Life.* Princeton: Aspen Institute for Humanistic Studies, 1978.

Edmonson, J. R., and Graham, D. M. "Animal Protein. Substitutes and Extenders." *Journal of Animal Science,* vol. 41, no. 2, 1975.

"Energy and Protein Requirements." Report of a Joint FAO/WHO Ad Hoc Expert Committee. Rome: FAO, 1973.

Ensminger, M. E., and Ensminger, Audrey. *China: The Impossible Dream.* Clovis, Calif.: Agri Services Foundation, 1973.

International Food Policy Research Institute. *Recent and Prospective Developments in Food Consumption: Some Policy Issues, Research Report 2.* Washington, D.C., July 1977.

World Food and Nutrition Study: Enhancement of Food Production for the United States. A report of the Board on Agriculture and Renewable Resources. Washington, D.C.: National Academy of Sciences, 1975.

World Food and Nutrition Study: The Potential Contributions of Research. Steering Committee, NRC Study on World Food and Nutrition of the Commission on International Relations. Washington, D.C.: National Academy of Sciences, 1977.

6

POLITICS

With each passing year, the poor throughout the world's developing countries sink deeper into poverty and face more frequent and prolonged periods of hunger and extreme malnutrition. They have become institutionalized into a culture of poverty.

In the absence of disruptive political crises, the percentage of the world's poor living in dire poverty is sure to increase unless the self-seeking political and economic motives of those who control production resources give way to policies based on commitments to improve the social and economic well-being of all.

It is not that the developing countries' plans have neglected employment opportunities or essential educational and health institutions and services for the poor. Plans have corroborated the need for the rural poor to have potable water, adequate housing, and "food enough" to meet minimal nutrition needs. When political leaders tour the countryside, they do not lack words expressing concern for the poor. However, since the poor are not organized, their cause must be espoused by political leaders outside their group who seldom feel deeply that poverty is a socioeconomic illness that must be eradicated.

CRITERIA. Five criteria have been selected to determine the strength of political commitment to improve the quality of life for all.

1. The commitments of political leaders should be rooted in political institutions.

As individuals, political leaders can advocate all kinds of nonsense and make promises having far-reaching implications for the poor. But the reality of politics dictates that until the plight of the poor becomes a priority of the political institutions, what individual political leaders say during campaigns and while on tours can be dismissed as mere political rhetoric.

Democracy and economic development are not contradictory

concepts. They are complementary concepts. Actually, economic development is political. Only when political institutions are responsible to the aspirations of the people will development serve the people.

2. Political leaders should influence legislatures to pass land and institutional reforms, or their promises are worthless.

The commitments of political institutions to make the nation's production resources more equitably available to the poor can be tested best by the type of reform legislation passed.

Since a large percentage of those elected to center and provincial legislative bodies come from families of substantial means with large landholdings, the passage of both land and institutional reforms requires political courage. In the past, the political risk in not passing these reforms was minimal. When one looks to the future, even within the next two decades, rising discontent and growing frustration over unfulfilled political promises indicate that the political risk trend will shift to support the cause of those living in poverty. Political leaders need to understand that effective land reforms contribute to justice and provide conditions for higher productivity.

3. Financial resources and scarce but competent manpower should be allocated to improve the quality of life for everyone.

A country that commits the bulk of its funds and assigns its most competent manpower to industrialization, defense, and urban services cannot claim to be giving priority to small-farm agriculture, family planning, and integrated rural development as the way to improve the level of living of the people.

4. The administrative bureaucracy should support the political commitment to improve the quality of life.

Political leaders can succeed in passing reform legislation and still fail the people if the administration is not fully supportive in implementing programs that flow from land and institutional reforms. A nation that speaks with two voices, one political and the other administrative, is a nation divided against itself.

5. Political leaders and administrators should emphasize the people's participation in program formulation and execution.

People's participation in all levels of planning program formulation and implementation is absolutely essential if the programs are to have lasting value in improving the way people live.

Political Action: Alternative Strategies. In the absence of population policies that will significantly reduce population growth, developing countries, can formulate and implement a wide range of economic and social policies and still fail to improve the quality of life of the people.

Now is the time for political leaders to act boldly, to commit themselves, and to get the support from political institutions for population policies to balance population with resources.

Obviously, the political commitment and muscle to carry out national policies and agricultural programs to increase production per hectare on small food-crop farms has been lacking during the past three decades. As a consequence, in-depth education of political leaders about the alternative development strategies and processes has been unfortunately neglected.

In the final analysis, the availability of production resources and how they are shared and used will determine the potential level of living the people may achieve. It is the balancing of population with resources that now requires the attention of all the political leaders in the Third World countries.

Furthermore, what the political leaders have lacked in the past thirty years has been the understanding that those living in poverty represent a potentially valuable development asset.

It is a safe prediction that in the future, hungry people will increasingly judge a government by the food that is has available for its people. In the present conflict, which is being fought on the unrealistic basis of ideologies, food supply is likely to be the deciding factor. One way or another, one-fourth of the world's population, representing one-half of the population in the developing countries, is bound to become a political force to be reckoned with in the decades ahead.

The alternative to giving priority to food-crop agriculture, rural development, and land and institutional reform programs is unrest, uprisings, political instability, and open revolutions.

It would be a mistake to end this discussion about the strategic importance of national policies supporting an egalitarian and just society backed by unqualified political support without adding a realistic qualification. Politics is an art; it is the art of getting elected and of staying in power. To be realistic, one should understand and accept that political decisions and political commitments are conditioned by numerous and conflicting interests. Politicians generally have two short-term objectives—to get elected and to stay in power.

Instead of faulting political leaders for being short-sighted and limited in their interests and commitments to here-and-now programs showing quick and visible results, a case is made for the continuous education of political leaders on the implications of alternative policies for the changes required to achieve national objectives. Development programs that are oriented toward people and institutions take far longer to achieve defined objectives than constructing a dam or building a plant to produce fertilizer.

The political leaders in the developing countries who are now making commitments to remove the conditions that create poverty and to provide employment opportunities in rural areas must understand that their commitments will require continuous political, administrative, and financial support on a priority basis over several decades.

To provide substance in educating political leaders about the time-consuming process of achieving national objectives, there will be a need for social research to provide the basis for formulating soundly conceived strategies for change.

While the poor still lack political clout, they are signaling a significant political message. They are not likely to continue exchanging their votes and political support for unfulfilled promises.

REFERENCES

Green, Daniel. *The Politics of Food.* Salisbury: Anchor Press, 1975.

Koirala, B. P. "We Are Abandoned." *Worldview,* Jan.-Feb. 1978.

Myrdal, Gunnar. *The Challenge of World Poverty: A World Anti-Poverty Program in Outline.* New York: Pantheon Books, 1970.

Orr, John Boyd, and Lubbock, David. *The White Man's Dilemma.* London: George Allen and Unwin, 1964.

Singh, Tarlok. "Alternative Forms of Agricultural Organization in Relation to Population Factors." In *Food Enough or Starvation for Millions,* edited by Douglas Ensminger. New Delhi: Tata McGraw-Hill, 1977.

Sinha, Radah. *Food and Poverty: The Political Economy of Confrontation.* London: Croom Helm, 1976.

7

TECHNOLOGY

Societies differ greatly in the way they are structured and how they function, giving each a distinctive culture. Culture is an organized, integrated system and can be divided into three subsystems: technological, sociological, and ideological. The technological system is composed of the material, mechanical, physical, and social elements, together with the institutions and their use. This system basically covers tools for production, means of subsistence, materials for shelter, institutional relations (formal and informal), and instruments of offense and defense.

TECHNOLOGY AND CULTURE. The technological system persistently plays an important role. Man has always been dependent on the material and mechanical means of adjustment to the natural environment. He has had to protect himself from the elements and to defend himself against enemies. He has also had to have sufficient amounts of food. He must do all these if he is to continue to live, and the only way he can meet his objective is through technological means. Therefore, the technological system is essential for man's survival.

In order for men to achieve their objectives, they must harness and control energy so that it will serve them. The functioning of culture rests upon and is determined by the amount of energy harnessed and by the way it is put to work. In general, sociologists contend that if all other factors are constant, culture evolves as the amount of energy harnessed per capita is increased, or as the efficiency of the tools of labor is increased.

Human energy was the first source of energy to be exploited by the earliest cultural systems. An average adult is capable of producing one-tenth of a horsepower. If women, children, the sick, and the aged are considered, the average power resources of the earliest cultures could be in the neighborhood of one-twentieth of horsepower per capita. Very few cultures have advanced rapidly by depending on human energy alone. Thus, even in early times, many cultures had to devise new ways to harness energy resources in order to advance beyond the limits of the energy resource of the human body. The conquest of fire was an early cultural achievement which was later converted to power the steam engine. The domestication of animals provided ancient cultures with more energy than did human muscle. Today mankind has more energy sources available in the form of coal, oil, natural gas, solar, and nuclear power.

The development of agricultural technology made profound change in early societies. Among western countries in the modern era, it was an essential component in the Industrial Revolution. Sources of raw materials became a major concern, and the scramble for colonies as suppliers of cheap raw materials took place. It was not long before the technological gap between the West and the colonies widened.

CHOICE OF TECHNOLOGY. Today the question of which technology to develop is an issue that concerns both developed and developing countries. While some industrial nations may think in terms of rocket shots to outer space, the concern of developing countries is for finding ways to feed and employ their poor. The right technology is crucial to the development aspirations of poor nations. These countries must choose the best way to combine their existing resources to address the misery of poverty and to form a broad base for future growth.

Various resources—land, capital and labor—have to be combined in the technologies adopted by the poor nations or for that matter, any nation. While in theory an optimum combination is always achieved, in practice, it is very difficult to optimize the use of these basic resources.

Determining which technology will be most effective is no simple matter. Political, economic, and managerial decisions as well as prestige, research, and development issues, and finally, the ease of transfer of technology from elsewhere are factors in the choice of an appropriate technology.

INDUSTRIALIZATION. After the decline of colonialism, an era emerged in which the newly independent nations believed the only way to advance was to emphasize large-scale industries, using high-level technology from the advanced industrialized nations. A marked degree of naiveté was demonstrated by the West and the poor developing countries in their belief that high-level technology was the answer. For a while, most of the developing nations thought they had an easy solution to their social and economic problems. The developed countries became deeply involved in selling their modern technology, while the poor nations went on a spending spree for this technology. But the industrialization policies of many poor nations have failed to produce economic growth for the majority of their people. Instead, they have been unable to achieve full employment and their policies have contributed to the rapid migration of people from rural areas to the cities. Thus at the moment, new alternatives are being encouraged.

A closer look at most of the developing nations will show why industrialization policies following the model of Western industrialized nations do not provide the impetus toward improving conditions for the poor. In most of these nations, the majority of the population is involved in agriculture. In Tanzania, for example, this majority means more than 95 percent of the people. It seems logical, therefore, that improvements in most developing nations should be made in the rural sector where most people live, rather than in the nonagricultural sector on the assumption that the benefits will "trickle down" to the majority. Perhaps this logic escaped the advocates of industrialization. The capital-intensive technology of the industrial nations is ill suited to the labor-surplus characteristic of developing countries.

The onset of "crash industrialization" led to the popular view that a relative working in an office in the city would earn more than he did when he worked on the plantation cultivating cassava, tea, or coffee. Many rural people moved to the cities hoping to gain employment. That the few capital-intensive industries would have been able to absorb the large number of city-life migrants is simply inconceivable. The net result is that many big cities in developing countries must face the problem of accommodating the unfortunates who fail to get the few available jobs. These people end up in the slums, adding to social problems and disease.

The problem is further compounded because those in the cities depend on the rural areas to provide their daily bread. The agricultural sector is unable to supply extra food except at rising prices because opportunities for agricultural expansion are not readily available. This leads to inflation and severe importation problems.

APPROPRIATE TECHNOLOGIES. Programs introduced to spur progress sometimes produce mixed blessings. Planners frequently overlook the possibility of unintended side effects, some favorable and some not. For example, those who master a new agricultural technology gain; but those who do not understand or adopt the new ways do not gain and, in fact, many become worse off. The resulting increase in gross national product may be accompanied by a widening economic gap between rich and poor. Both favorable and unfavorable side effects of agricultural development programs need to be identified, and companion programs need to be devised to achieve balanced growth.

Criteria. What is clearly needed in these nations is a technology that will benefit all the people. Such a technology will mean that the sellers and recipients of technology first of all have a clear understanding of their priorities, environments, and people. Such an appreciation could prevent repetition of tragic mistakes. Appropriate technology, as it is presently viewed, encompasses technology for a modern steel mill, a large commercial farm, a small village industry, and a small subsistence food-crop farmer. For the modern steel mill and the large commercial farm, the emphasis would be on the application of advanced technology. For the small village industry or the subsistence food-crop farmer, technology oriented to the resources of the small industrialist and small farmer, within the managerial competence of both, should be developed and applied.

If technology is to be approriate to the needs of the developing countries it should be initiated and implemented in those countries. To be appropriate for application, the technology must respect ethical values, the environment, and the resources available as well as managerial competence.

Mahatma Gandhi's View. It is interesting to note that the present emphasis on appropriate technology closely parallels the philosophy and teaching of Mahatma Gandhi, the architect of the Indian independence movement. Because of his interest and support for village and rural development programs in India, Gandhi was forever searching for and experimenting with new technology. But Gandhi was persistent in his insistence that the technology he sought meet two criteria: it should be of benefit to most people; and the technology should be within the managerial competence and available resources of most people. Mahatma Gandhi, quoted in E. G. Vallianatos's *Fear in the Countryside: The Control of Agricultural Resources in the Poor Countries by Nonpeasant Elites* (1976), wrote:

What I object to is the craze for machinery, not machinery as such. The craze is for what they call labour-saving machinery. Men go on 'saving labour' till thousands are without work and thrown on the streets to die of starvation. I want to save time and labour, not for a fraction of mankind, but for all. I want the concentration of wealth, not in the hands of a few, but in the hands of all. Today machinery helps a few to ride on the backs of millions. The impetus behind it is not the philanthropy to save labour, but greed.

INAPPROPRIATE TECHNOLOGIES. The lack of understanding by the suppliers of technology is exemplified by the case of the large-scale British project near Dodoma, in what was then Tanganyika. At the end of World War II when the West lost the transoceanic countries, England looked to East Africa to provide the deliveries formerly supplied by India and Indonesia. A project to grow ground nuts, involving 3.2 million acres, was drawn at an investment of $25 million, and it mobilized all types of experts.

The project was intended in part to demonstrate how modern and better methods work. In a way it was criticism of how the African peasant worked his soil. Bulldozers were brought to remove trees, taking longer than had been anticipated by the planners. This clearing effort exposed the soil to wind and rain and led to serious erosion of the precious humus layer, whose depth had been overestimated initially. The exposed soil became hard, so that the seeds could not germinate. Artificial fertilizer did not prove to be very effective because of the lack of water. The net result was that the yield fell far below the yield of the simple African farmer. After six years of struggle, the project was finally stopped. The capital outlay was one hundred million dollars.

"INTERMEDIATE TECHNOLOGY." Drawing heavily on Gandhi's philosophy that technology must be applicable to people with limited resources and traditional ways, Dr. E. F. Schumacher, in his book, *Small Is Beautiful: Economics As If People Mattered,* has focused worldwide attention on the need of developing countries for an appropriate technology.

In his search for appropriate technology, Schumacher seems to have fused together the necessary conditions for what he calls "intermediate technology." He proposes that:

1. Workplaces be created in the areas where the people are living now, and not primarily in the metropolitan areas into which they tend to migrate.

2. These workplaces must be, on average, cheap enough so that they can be created in large numbers without this calling for an unattainable level of capital formation and imports.

3. The production methods employed must be relatively simple, so that the demands for high skills are minimized, not only in the production process itself but also in matters of organization, raw material supply, financing, marketing, and so forth.

4. Production should be mainly from local materials and mainly for local use.

Regional. Schumacher has stated the issue of appropriate technology in a clear and solid form. Technology, he insists, must be viewed from a regional standpoint. Poor nations must first be prepared to admit that the quality of goods they use need not be comparable to those required by a developed nation. Past and current trends in many of these nations show that if a higher quality can be used, it will be adopted without delay. Obviously, these high quality goods can only be bought by a few because of their price tags.

Efficiency Measurement. Efficiency in the West is normally evaluated by measuring output per worker. This is a logical procedure since labor in the West is a scarce resource. In the poor nations a more appropriate way of measuring efficiency should be based on an evaluation of the output per unit cost of the inputs of capital and labor.

Scarcity and Pricing. Despite an abundance of labor in the developing nations, union organizations have been able to secure minimum wages, fringe benefits, and higher wages than would ordinarily prevail in an area with similar labor resources. At the same time capital, which is in short supply, tends to be heavily subsidized. It is accorded low interest rates, preferential tariffs, accelerated depreciation allowances, tax holidays, and is over valued in foreign exchange. These factors should be considered carefully by the poor nations. Government action, whether intentional or unintentional, determines whether it will be more favorable for capital-intensive or labor-intensive technology. Government action would make the concept of appropriate technology utilization less systematic. The ideal way to choose an appropriate technology is to imitate a system in which the prices of the factors of production reflect their relative scarcities in the particular economy.

RESEARCH AND TECHNOLOGY TRANSFER. While it seems safe to conclude there is wide acceptance at the policy level by both developed and developing countries that future emphasis should be on appropriate technology, it would be naive to assume that research institutions are presently staffed by people who have the aptitudes and motivations to do the kind of research essential to a technology aimed at small industries and small food-crop farmers.

Research Priorities. Given this historical perspective in technological transfer and the emerging shift in emphasis from industrialization and capital-intensive projects to rural development, small, dispersed economic enterprises, small-farm food-crop agriculture, and labor-intensive projects, developing countries urgently need to create new research institutions and make major changes in existing ones to assure the development of appropriate technology. There will be a few exceptions where the appropriate technology cannot be better developed within the countries where it is to be applied.

In this shift from transfer of advanced technology to within-country development, there will still be a role for the developed countries to play. The "know-how" to relate research to needs and to develop technology to meet specific future requirements will be the developed countries' major technological contribution to the developing countries.

Social Technology. This brings to the forefront the idea that further research should be as concerned about social technology as it has been about production-oriented technology. While all too limited, there is more production technology than social technology.

All countries with five-year plans tend to limit their activities to setting goals and allocating resources. There is a need for planning to achieve specified goals. Even if there is acceptance of the proposed change, the social technology to give it meaning does not exist.

If one admits that all development takes place through people and their institutions, a strong case can be made for major investments in social technology. There is little solid social research that provides an understanding of the processes involved in transforming traditional societies and in integrating the poor majority into the social and cultural fabric of the nation. While there is a considerable body of production-orientated research for formulating agricultural production programs, there is limited social technology to demonstrate alternative ways to organize small landholdings into group-farm structures. All too little is known about the decision-making process involved in the small-farm family finally accepting, applying, and integrating new technology into the farm work schedule and the family pattern of living.

Although it is easy to talk about improving the quality of life, very little is known about what the people living in poverty regard as their most precious values. Research into the priority values of people who live in poverty is imperative.

While there is a consensus that there is a need to develop an institutional infrastructure with which small-farm food-crop farmers can identify that will serve the needs of small farms, there is only limited institutional research within the developing countries to provide guidance in the development of appropriate and urgently needed institutions.

Institutional Structures. In the process of giving and receiving agricultural technical assistance during the past thirty years, great emphasis was placed on transferring the United States structure of cooperative institutional arrangements to the developing countries. These arrangements involved the United States Department of Agriculture and the colleges of agriculture of the land-grant universities, and their conduct of research in agricultural technology for extension programs for the farmers. The wisdom of transferring proven United States agricultural research, teaching, extension institutions, and methods to the developing countries was seldom questioned. Now, thirty years later, and after the United States agricultural extension institutional models have been widely transplanted throughout the developing countries, the evidence is overwhelming that the extension structure and especially the methods that worked so well to serve American agriculture were seldom suited to the needs and cultures of the developing countries.

Upon reflection, one realizes that the mistake was in the transfer of the structure and methods as they functioned in the development of a market-oriented, commercial, and scientific United States agriculture. What should have been transferred by the United States agricultural structure was the philosophy of serving the needs of the farmers.

Those leaders in the transfer of such agricultural institutions failed to appreciate that in the beginning stages of the development of land-grant college research and extension programs, the college staff went directly to the farmers to learn what their problems and needs were. The farmers' problems provided the basis for research priorities. These findings were then taken to the farmer by the extension staff, and the farmers were assisted in its application.

When, in the application of the new technology, the farmer required new institutions, whether in marketing or credit, the extension staff of the colleges provided the leadership to organize these essential institutions. At each and every stage of change and development of American agriculture, the land-grant universities provided the leadership and technology. Since all developing countries are confronted with inadequate and ill-suited institutions, research should provide guidance on institutional structures and their functions.

ORGANIZATIONAL AND INSTITUTIONAL REFORM. In recent years, increasing attention has been focused on identifying the constraints that inhibit the acceptance of technology for agriculture and rural development. There are many instances where either the absence of institutions or the presence of traditional and inappropriate institutions have been identified as two of the most important deterrents against the acceptance of available, trustworthy technology.

Whereas the decades of the sixties and seventies can be recognized as the period when priority was given to developing networks of national and international agricultural research institutions, the decade of the eighties must highlight and stress the creation of institutions to transmit the technology and especially institutions for servicing small-farm agriculture and rural development. This does not imply that there should be any weakening of support for research. Research must be a continuous process searching for more appropriate technology and better answers to the complete range of agricultural and rural development problems.

When making a case for developing institutional infrastructures that promote small-farm agriculture and rural development, it would be naive and inaccurate to assume that there is an abundance of social technology presently available. New institutions create a sound basis for a beginning, but social research must provide the social technology for progressive institutional development. This concept ought to be accepted in the same way we accept the research institutions that provide agricultural production technology.

In deciding whether or not to create entirely new institutions or to attempt to transfer existing institutions, one must first be prepared to answer the following questions: What kind of institutions? What functions need to be performed? and Which targeted population groups will they serve? When evaluating institutions, one should bear in mind that they have the potential either to perpetuate the status quo or to facilitate change. The objective in organization should be to create an institutional infrastructure to solve problems relevant to the environment in which they occur.

Because of the limited purposes for which most institutions were created during the colonial era, few developing countries have succeeded in transforming their institutions to perform as catalysts for change in a developing socioeconomy. The greatest constraint in transforming institutions that were dominant during the colonial era is that these institutions were originally created to serve the export and cash crops of large-farm and plantation agriculture. There will be few exceptions where traditional, large-scale farming-dominated institutions of the colonial era can be transformed to serve small-farm agriculture and rural development.

Rural Poor. Down through the ages, the rural poor have existed outside formal organizations, institutions, and government policies. Since they have had to fend for themselves, survival, not development, has been their dominant value. Large and medium farmers have looked to the organizations and institutions which they dominate to assist them in modernizing their agriculture, but small farmers, village tradesmen, and landless laborers have had to rely on traditionalism and the local moneylender.

When families operating small farms follow traditional agricultural practices, as most of them do, the family as a unit is totally involved in farming. Under traditional agriculture, traditions provide the basis for practices, not new technology. When credit is needed, it is the traditional moneylender who can be counted upon. Under traditional and subsistence agriculture, the land is expected to produce enough to meet minimum family needs. Modern agriculture, which is geared to maximizing production, is oriented toward marketing in addition to family needs.

When small farmers move from traditional and subsistence agriculture toward modernized agriculture, they are dependent on a wide range of organizations, institutional services, and government policies beyond the family. The new agricultural technology can be successfully applied and integrated into a new family pattern of work only if the requisite organizations, institutions, and services exist and are trustworthy.

Because the rural poor are not organized, whatever programs formulated to benefit them the past thirty years have been administered programs. These administered programs sought the people's participation and cooperation. However, the people who were to benefit were not organized to lead or to make the decisions. Few government programs for the poor have successfully moved to the rural poor through established organizations, institutions, and administrations.

When one looks back over the past thirty years of administered poverty programs, it is difficult to find evidence of lasting benefits. Substantial sums of money have been spent on poverty-related programs, but no significant organizations and institutions have been created to institutionalize the methods and processes of involving the poor in programs of economic improvement and social betterment. The literature on social change provides abundant evidence that lasting change comes from popular participation in trustworthy organizations and institutions and not from without by superimposed administered programs.

Along with government policies and specific programs for the benefit of the rural poor, government should be responsible for programs to ensure that the benefits do in fact reach the rural poor. Government programs for credit and inputs in agriculture and rural enterprises are good examples of such administrative support.

As long as farm and rural organizations, most of which are quasi-government institutions, are dominated by large and medium farmers and are used by government as the main channels for credit and agricultural inputs to farmers, the small farmer's needs will remain unmet.

But this is only half the story. The established organizations and institutions have little to offer the most destitute poverty groups—the landless laborers, the very small farmers, the village artisans, and other rural groups in poverty.

The existence of the poor majority outside established organizations and institutions goes far toward explaining why this sector of the population has had little influence over national policies. They lack established channels for communicating with government and political institutions and they are not organized to help themselves. Also, research institutions do not look upon the rural poor as having researchable needs.

While the majority of the rural poor are still illiterate, they are intelligent enough to see for themselves that those who control the production resources and institutions are benefiting from government development programs. In scattered instances throughout the Third World countries the poor have joined in movements to assert their rights. When one looks for significant change in rural areas—the growing assertiveness of the poor—certainly the by-passed people stand out as signaling that change is on the way.

So we come to the basic question, not should the rural poor be organized, but rather should a government committed to eradicating poverty commit itself to providing leadership in organizing the rural poor in the same way people's cooperatives would be organized? It is safe to conclude that in one way or another the rural poor will be organized. Governments can either decide to provide the leadership for this sector of the population to develop constructively, or wait until they are organized to carry out revolutionary programs.

The objectives and means by which the rural poor are to be organized should be decided now. Who will organize the rural poor should be a political decision. But the organizations, institutions, and leadership created to serve them must not be politically partisan. There should be unqualified agreement that the main objective in organizing the rural poor is to provide for their economic advancement and social achievement.

The widely differing population groups that constitute the rural poor will be far more easily organized into meaningful and appropriate institutional structures in a rural/urban community. Resistance and hostility expressed by the elite for poverty-related programs can be expected to disturb the status quo and challenge the domination of the elite. Unless the poor are organized for economic advancement and social achievement, it will be difficult, if not impossible, to reverse the trend toward further institutionalization of the elite minority and the poor majority.

REFERENCES

Agricultural Technology for Developing Nations: Farm Mechanization Alternatives for 1–10 Hectare Farms. Proceedings of Special International Conference, University of Illinois at Urbana-Champaign, May 22–24, 1978.

Alternatives to Growth '77, The Nature of Growth in Equitable and Sustainable Societies, Oct. 2–4, 1977, Woodlands, Texas.

Blase, Melvin G. *Institution Building: A Source Book.* Ann Arbor, Mich.: LithoCrafters, 1973.

Food and Agriculture Issue. *Scientific American,* Sept. 1976.

Norman, D. W., and Krishnaswamy, M. S. "The Adoption of Improved Technology by the Small Farmer." In *Food Enough or Starvation for Millions,* edited by Douglas Ensminger. New Delhi: Tata McGraw-Hill, 1977.

Schumacher, E. F. *Small Is Beautiful: Economics As If People Mattered.* Scranton, Pa.: Harper & Row, 1973.

Stout, B. A., and Downing, Charles M. "Increasing Productivity of Human, Animal and Engine Power." In *Food Enough or Starvation for Millions,* edited by Douglas Ensminger. New Delhi: Tata McGraw-Hill, 1977.

Thomas, D. Woods; Potter, Harry; Miller, William F.; and Aveni, Adrian F. *Institution Building: A Model for Applied Social Change.* Cambridge, Mass.: Schenkman, 1972.

8

SMALL-FARM AGRICULTURE
AND RURAL DEVELOPMENT

When one understands where the Third World countries started their development journey thirty years ago, lacking experience, trained manpower, and financial resources, and possessing precious little technology appropriate to small-farm food-crop agriculture, it is to their credit that by the end of the seventies they have achieved an average annual growth of 2.7 percent. The issue is not about what has been achieved, but rather what changes in policies and development strategies must be adopted by the developing countries if they are to increase their production to 4 percent per annum as recommended by the United Nations' Food and Agriculture Organization. A 4 percent growth in agricultural production will be required if the developing countries are to meet the nutritional needs of a population growing at an annual rate of 1.7 percent at mid-1979. An examination of how the developing countries have approached agriculture reveals weak political policies and an institutional infrastructure too inadequate to serve small-farm food-crop and livestock agriculture. Since its formation, following the 1974 World Food Conference, the United Nations' World Food Council has repeatedly expressed concern that food production, particularly in the food priority countries, is growing much more slowly in this decade of the seventies than in the 1960s. Dramatic food shortages continue to exist in a large number of developing countries in Africa and South Asia; the number of undernourished people increased from 400 million at the end of the 1960s, to 800 million by the end of the 1970s, and almost all this increase has been in the food priority countries.

Instead of a comprehensive program approach to increasing agriculture production, the most commonly followed strategy has been to single out particular aspects of agriculture for emphasis. Technology, institutions, and services have met, with few exceptions, the needs of the medium and large farmers and have largely by-passed the small food-crop farmers. There have been few attempts to develop technology into a package of practices for the small food-crop farmer or for the early development of effective institutions and services specifically oriented to them. All countries have lacked needed financial resources to support an integrated approach to agricultural development. In addition, the medium and large farmers have more political clout. Consequently, they command more of the production resources, dominate the time of the extension services staff, and have first call on the limited strategic agricultural inputs—improved seed, fertilizer, credit, and water.

If the major recommendation of the United Nations World Food Conference—that developing countries give the highest priority to increasing production on small farms—is to be achieved, substantial additional funds for research and a greatly stepped-up program to train agricultural scientists to man the research institutions will be needed. A major constraint in the modernization of small-farm agriculture for developing countries is their lack of appropriate production and social technology.

INTEGRATED AGRICULTURAL DEVELOPMENT. Based on the developing countries' experience in increasing production per hectare on small food-crop farms during the past thirty years, it can be concluded that if the developing countries wish to increase agricultural production from the present and persistent trend of 2.7 percent up to 4 percent per annum, they will have to accept an integrated approach to agricultural development. Through an integrated approach, all things related to agricultural production and rural development would be identified and interrelated in national policies and programs.

As can be seen from Figure 8.1, an integrated approach to agriculture is made up of thirteen interrelated and interdependent parts. The strength of the farmers and how they relate to the programs will determine which farmers (large, small, or both) respond to the recommended new technology and integrate it into their work schedules. To be acceptable, this new technology must become a part of the family pattern of living, which allows time for priority cultural activities such as weddings and festivals.

In advocating an integrated approach to agriculture, it would be wrong to conclude that all thirteen parts could or should be added from the beginning. The working of the program will signal when an additional area will provide momentum to the development process. An understanding of the culture and economy of the area and of the

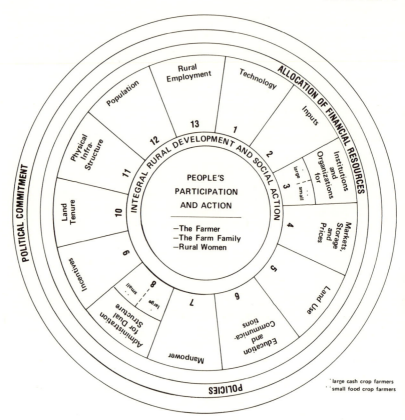

Fig. 8.1. A Systems Approach to Agricultural Development

immediate objectives to be achieved should help select the priority areas to be built into the program initially.

It seems a safe assumption that weak political commitment, insufficient funding, inadequate institutions, limited technology appropriate for small farmers, land tenure patterns, and administrative incompetence may well be the determining factors in limiting agricultural production on the small farms. Graphically speaking, political commitment, policies, and allocation of financial resources are the rims of the wheel; people's participation and integrated agricultural and rural development are the wheel's hub; and the thirteen specific program areas are the spokes. Together, they constitute a total program.

The thirteen program parts provide content, incentives, minimize risk, contribute to the farmer's adoption of the new technology, and help adapt it to his farm work schedule as well as to the family work pattern and cultural activities. Since these thirteen parts are like the spokes of a wheel—all essential—then policies, appropriate programs, and funding for each must be included in an integrated approach to agricultural and rural development.

PROGRAM AREAS. With few exceptions, the research institutions in the developing countries have only now begun to develop technology for small food-crop farm and livestock agriculture that is oriented to the resource base and the level of managerial competence of small farms. Little thought has been given in the past as to whether or not the recommended technology is economically feasible or relevant to the farm work schedule (W. Klatt, "Causes and Cures of Agrarian Unrest in Asia." *Southeast Asian Spectrum,* 1974). There is also a void in applicable agricultural technology for the 85 percent of the world's limited-moisture agriculture that is rain fed. Lacking is a technology specifically tailored to the needs of the one-acre to five-acre farmer.

Most of the small-farm food-crop and livestock agriculture is rain fed with limited and uncertain moisture; thus future research emphasis should be on tillage practices that are both water and soil conservative. Present tillage and grazing practices keep the soil bare and prevent much of the limited rain from entering the soil. Required are tillage practices that retain a residue on the surface to enhance water entering the soil and maintain moisture for plant growth.

In the future, the agricultural research emphasis must be oriented to the nation's commitment to policies and programs that are labor-intensive. And it is essential that the technology be appropriate. It should be oriented to the farmer's resources of varying sizes and levels of managerial competence and be supportive of labor-intensive agriculture.

Inputs. The recommended technology determines the kind of inputs that must be available to the farmers. Government policies must assure the high quality of the recommended inputs and their accessibility to all farmers at the time and in the amounts required.

Credit is a strategically important input for a small food-crop development strategy. Without credit, the small farmers will not be able to procure the recommended inputs, especially improved seed, fertilizer, and pesticides. Increasing investments will be a prerequisite for the development and distribution of irrigation systems, especially for small-farm food-crop agriculture.

Since small-farm food-crop and livestock agriculture is largely on a subsistence basis, and because a large percentage of the tillers are tenants and/or operators of small holdings, a completely new approach to determine credit worthiness is essential. If the small farmers are to be consistent users of credit, government policies will have to assure refinancing of loans when there are crop losses from adverse weather conditions.

Furthermore, the rising cost of energy inputs derived from oil, especially fertilizers, are likely to be even further out of the price range of the small-acre farmer. This will present a dilemma to governments. They will have to choose between subsidizing the costly energy inputs to agriculture or increasing their foreign exchange earnings to import food grains.

Institutions and Organizations. Institutions and organizations must exist or else be created to serve agriculture's needs. However, the orientation and commitment of the institutions and organizations determine whether or not they serve all farmers or cater to only the large farmers. Special attention must be given to creating new institutions and organizations suitable to small-farm food-crop and livestock agriculture.

If institutions and farmer organizations are to serve both the nation and the farmer, they must foster two-way communication. Government, through institutions, informs people about national policies and priorities and seeks farmer cooperation. Similarly, it is through institutions and farmer organizations that farmers' problems, services, and recommended national farm policies are communicated to the government.

The aspirations of the present landless laborers and holders of small units to achieve a higher and more secure level of living require that each country examine alternative forms of group farming and select the one best suited to its culture and economy. Farming arrangements are needed to make fuller application of advanced technology, management, and irrigation possible.

Farmers of small units must look to their land to produce food for their families, in contrast to the large farmers who produce for a market. Obviously, a new political attitude should be considered—one that encourages and assists farmers in developing an intensive garden-type agriculture. The objective should be to assist farmers of small holdings to improve both the quality and quantity of food for family consumption. Thus a positive step will have been taken by millions of people, now living in poverty, to achieve a minimally nutritional diet. In moving this group of small landholders toward intensive garden agriculture, research institutions and extension staffs concerned about intensive garden agriculture are required.

Separate cooperatives should be formed by the landless laborers and the small landholders, who have more in common with each other than they do with the medium and large farmers. Having their own cooperatives gives better assurance that credit will be available for organizing their own economic enterprises as well as for providing custom services.

Markets, Storage, and Prices. Trustworthy markets, easily accessible to farmers, contribute to the transition from a largely subsistence traditional agriculture toward a food-producing agriculture, providing more food for family needs and even leaving some for the market.

The development of local markets has been neglected during the past thirty years. The farmer's decision to risk credit and invest in agricultural inputs has been powerfully influenced by the presence of markets and his early experiences with them. Government agricultural price policies, through the marketing institutional system, must be implemented at the farmer's level. Whereas in the past, the agricultural price policies of the developing countries have been urban-consumer oriented, the future policies must be producer oriented. The farmer's experience in selling at his local market will greatly influence his decision on whether or not to take the risk and apply the new technology.

All developing countries face a dilemma in working out agricultural price policies. Political leaders face two very real conflicts in setting price policies that will be acceptable to urban consumers and farmers who cannot afford to risk investments without floor-price guarantees.

Because urban consumers tend to be highly volatile politically, agricultural price policies in the developing countries in the past have favored them. Mounting pressures for the developing countries to increase production per hectare on the small food-crop farms will force political leaders in the future to institute price policies that provide for production incentives or subsidies on inputs and credit.

To balance the political tension which surely will emerge from higher food prices, political leaders will want to examine policies to subsidize either the urban consumer to hold prices low, or the farmer producer to make production more profitable. Some countries have subsidized limited-income people by issuing cards entitling them to buy at government fair-priced shops.

Storage facilities are of major importance in a government policy designed to build up grain reserves. Because of the high cost of building storage facilities using proven technology and because of the large sums of money tied up in purchasing grain for storage, few countries presently believe they can afford to set aside more funds than those required to meet immediate emergencies. But some storage facilities should be included in each country's agricultural development plan. Safe and adequate storage facilities within the community will minimize losses from storage as well as serve as an incentive for the small farmers to produce some crops for market.

Grain in storage can contribute to the stabilization of prices for producer as well as for the consumer. But grain held in storage should never be used to suppress prices for the producer below production cost.

Land Use. On a worldwide basis, it is no exaggeration to say that if the potentially productive land not now in cultivation were added to all the present cultivated land, and if the land were then used for the most suitable crops, all the world's people could be provided with a nutritionally adequate diet today and beyond the year 2000. Since this possibility is not likely to approach reality within the foreseeable future, common sense requires that we examine land-use policies that have the potential of being accepted politically and made operational.

There are at least eight land-use options open to most of the developing countries that offer promise for increasing agricultural production. They are:

1 Increase production per hectare on present farm units. Special attention should be given to moving the very small farm units to intensive and garden-type agriculture.

2. Bring more land under cultivation.

3. Examine the advantages and disadvantages of converting land presently devoted to producing export crops to producing food crops.

4. Break up large holdings into viable economic units using labor-intensive technology and methods.

5. Increase the acreage under irrigation to make possible more crop-intensive farming.

6. Change existing cropping patterns in areas where soil, water, and climate are supportive of high yields.

7. Change from traditional single cropping to multi- and inter-cropping.

8. Develop marginal land into productive land.

For many countries, it would be good economics as well as sound land-use policy to grow crops for export when the economic advantage is enough to provide a margin of profit. They could then use the earned foreign exchange to import the country's deficit food needs.

Largely because internal transportation and communication both within and between regions of many of the developing countries were either limited or nonexistent in the colonial era, each sought to be self-sufficient in food. Thus for many areas and regions, this has meant that crops are being grown that are not best suited to the area. But major area and regional shifts in land use will require research to answer the question, What crops are best suited? Institutions and markets oriented to the new crops will have to be developed. Farmer education will have to be intense to carry him through several cropping cycles.

Livestock, Poultry, and Fisheries. By giving high priority to the production of livestock, poultry, and fisheries when developing farming and cropping systems, family income can be substantially increased and a more balanced diet assured. When a comprehensive approach is taken to livestock, poultry, and fisheries production programs, these enterprises can become the major source of income for landless laborers and farmers whose holdings are very small. A comprehensive approach includes research and application of technology, a trustworthy market, and all supporting services, including credit.

Since most of the agricultural research for the past three decades has emphasized the cultivation of crops, both for food and exports, a higher priority in the future will be needed for research on livestock, poultry, and fisheries. Research will provide guidance on which livestock, poultry, or fisheries programs are potentially profitable. Although it will be important to give greater emphasis to the development of these enterprises, some restraint should be exercised until plans have been formulated to either create new institutions or transfer old ones that provide the services essential for a successful livestock, poultry, or fisheries enterprise.

Education. Since all decisions related to farming are made by the farmer and his family, it seems inconceivable that the importance of education in applying scientific methods to improve traditional agriculture and to introduce new technology has been given so little prominence. Yet to change toward a food-producing agriculture, farmers should be able to reason, understand interrelations, analyze problems, weigh alternative solutions, and make decisions that will minimize risk.

Assuming that the farmer is central to the nation's aim of increasing production per hectare, the farmer should be encouraged to become a resourceful human being, capable of understanding the new technology. He should know how to organize, manage, and fit this technology into both his pattern of farm work and his pattern of family living.

Manpower. All developing countries continue to face major manpower shortages, especially in areas where technical, administrative, and managerial competence are required.

With the emphasis now shifting from transference of advanced technology to creation of appropriate technology within the countries, there is an observable shift away from training abroad to training within the developing countries.

Administration and Management. The way an administration responds to the needs of the people is the best test of its effectiveness. As programs succeed and bring credit to political leadership, political support grows. When there is neither a meaningful political commitment nor effective administration, traditional subsistence agriculture can be expected to continue unchanged.

The evidence is overwhelming that agricultural administration in the developing countries is presently catering to the needs of the medium and large market, cash-crop farmers. This strengthens the case for an independent but coordinated administration to serve the needs of a small-farm food-producing agriculture. To overhaul the colonial administrative structure now appears to be hopeless.

Incentives. Examination of the various forms of organizing agriculture for production throughout the world reveals that when individual initiative and extra work are rewarded, an increase in production follows.

But the farmer's response is weak to national appeals to increase production in order to feed all its people. Farmers do not respond to slogans relating their increased efforts to patriotism. We also know farmers seldom respond to government-assigned targets that specify the technology to be applied for a given crop on a specified number of hectares.

Price policies which are producer oriented are a significant incentive to the larger and medium-size farmers who have resources and managerial skills to apply new technological inputs. For the small, subsistence food-crop farmers, the incentives to relate the application of new technology, and to farm more intensely to increase production as a means of achieving an improved level of living have been overlooked. It could prove to be the most positive of all stimuli for the small food-crop farmers to want to improve their traditional agricultural practices and to integrate new technology into their farm work schedule and family pattern of living.

Land Tenure. Few problems haunt the political leaders of developing countries more persistently than land tenure arrangements. While many countries have formulated, debated, and most have passed some form of land tenure legislation, little has been changed to improve the economic potential of tenants, landless laborers, and holders of small units.

If the developing countries enforce the 1974 World Food Conference recommendation that increased production per hectare on small farms be stressed, implementing realistic land tenure legislation becomes urgent.

Physical Infrastructure. While plans must be formulated early to build roads, railroads, irrigation systems, and transport systems, great care and constraint must be exercised in carrying out the plans. Preference should be given to establishing links between all major agricultural producing regions and between the regions and the national center. Since the construction of the physical infrastructure is part of an integrated approach, funding should be justified in terms of getting agricultural inputs to the farmers and the farmers' produce to the markets.

Population. Agriculture has the responsibility for producing enough food to meet the nutritional needs of all the people. Thus agricultural policies should include support for population policies. Naturally, ministers of agriculture should be concerned about national population policies and family plans to limit population growth.

While it is not assumed that the ministry of agriculture should be engaged in promoting family planning, it is assumed that agriculture should add information for farm families to its educational extension programs stressing that agriculture is approaching the upper limits of its ability to cope with unchecked population growth. Agricultural field workers are in close contact with rural people and can influence the farm family to understand that they should limit the number of children so all can be nutritionally well fed.

Employment in Rural Areas. Future emphasis must be on labor-intensive technology to increase employment opportunities within agriculture. While agriculture must bear the larger responsibility for employment of the rural labor force, it alone cannot provide the jobs for all who are partially employed or unemployed. Since agricultural demands on labor are seasonal, rural employment must be organized to support agricultural labor needs.

Rural public works programs can be justified when they strengthen the economic base. Such rural works programs as an irrigation system, land leveling, contouring to reduce soil erosion, and construction of farm-to-market roads will enhance agricultural development.

If advances are to be made in improving yields on the small food-producing farms, the significance of the conservation of traditions should be appreciated. They are like ancient walls built around palaces that keep the outside world away and preserve the hard earned treasures within.

While we should not seek to destroy this wall, we should seek to penetrate it from within to understand the mind of the small farmer. Only as we do so may we realize that although traditions sometimes are obstacles to progress, at other times they are foundations for change.

INTEGRATED RURAL DEVELOPMENT. Integrated rural development must have two corollary objectives—to integrate the rural poor into the national cultural fabric and to coordinate and direct all rural development programs toward the creation of socioeconomically viable rural/urban communities.

Rural/Urban Communities. A socioeconomically viable rural/urban community is an area where a growth center, institutions, services, and major markets are located, and where people from the surrounding areas go to purchase farm and family supplies and goods; where a wide range of employment opportunities in addition to agriculture are obtainable; where the native born can look forward to education, medical services, residence, and earning a living in the area; and where socioeconomic services and cultural programs comparable to those found in the urban areas are available to all. Its population will range from fifteen to fifty thousand. Public works programs to develop farm-to-market hard surface roads, linking the outlying areas to the growth center will provide employment and contribute to a sense of community.

Through the fostering of socially and economically sound rural/urban communities, an institutional process can be started that will generate increasing numbers of employment opportunities over time. A second equally important process will be the growth of institutions, socioeconomic services, and cultural programs. As these rural/urban communities develop, the people in the rural areas will experience greater employment possibilities in the rural areas than exist in the urban centers. The effect will be a slowing of the migration trend from rural to urban areas, thus stabilizing the population in rural areas. This will contribute to solving the growing overpopulation crisis of the cities, brought on by the migration of rural people who move to the cities searching for employment.

Objectives. Based on thirty years of worldwide rural development experience, some of the specific objectives achievable through integrated rural development can be stated:

1. Remove the conditions contributing to rural poverty and broaden the base of employment for the unemployed and partially employed.

2. Develop a food-producing agriculture following scientific methods with special emphasis on small-farm subsistence agriculture.

3. Develop both physical, formal, and informal socioeconomic institutional infrastructures to serve the people.

4. Balance population growth with resources essential to raising the nutritional quality of diets and improving the level of living of everyone.

5. Provide, within rural areas, a variety of socioeconomic services and cultural programs that are comparable in quality to services of urban areas.

6. Stimulate and promote a sense of community, concern, and pride in achievement.

7. Transform the educational system by stressing community education and the development of self-respect.

8. Foster policies, plans, and program strategies that will provide balanced growth, giving special attention to the poorer regions and the neglected weaker yet vulnerable sectors of the population.

Today, on a worldwide basis, we have available the past thirty years of rural and community development experience. The question is whether present leaders and advocates of rural development will have the patience and time to draw on this vast experience or will they again go their own way, rely on their judgments, and in doing so, rediscover much of what is already known?

Guidelines. Some of the more important lessons to be drawn from the past thirty years of rural development experience in the developing countries are:

1. Be specific about the terms of reference for integrated rural development for creating an egalitarian society that will assure those now locked in poverty that they can contribute and share.

Development must first have a space dimension, encompassing a geographic area and population group large enough for the redirection of the total area as a socioeconomic and politically viable rural/urban community.

2. State clearly the objectives to be achieved through a nationally integrated development program: integrate the rural poor into the national culture fabric and create socioeconomic and politically viable rural/urban communities.

3. Decentralize the appropriate administrative subdivision below the state/provincial level.

Decentralization should mean complete decentralization of administration and the creation of a legal institution through which people, either by direct or indirect elections, assume leadership for planning, development, and implementation of all programs and activities.

One highly qualified government officer should have complete charge of all staff and coordinate all center and state funds expended within the administrative decentralized area.

At the administrative subdivisional level, provisions must be made to assure adequate representation of both men and women, geographically and socioeconomically, in the election of the people's representatives.

4. Unqualified political support backed by effectively implemented land and institutional reform legislation is essential.

5. Education for self-reliance must play an important role in developing people as the nation's most important resource.

6. A strong economic base will be one of the crucial factors in determining the success of integrated rural development. First priority should be given to agriculture and agriculture-related enterprises and activities, but a wide range of employment-focused programs will need to be fostered including public works, crafts, small industries, and services.

7. Substantial government funds will be required, and the test of the strength of political commitment to remove the conditions that create poverty can be measured by the adequacy of funds budgeted for integrated rural development.

There should be no illusion about either the magnitude and complexity of the task or the time required to integrate the cultures of the elite minority and the poor majority into one national culture. The evolution of political institutions committed to the advancement of the people will increasingly become a reality as the poor majority organize and the political power base shifts from the elite minority to the poor majority, as it is in the process of doing.

The long-range national objective of integrated rural development should be to provide the conditions for a just, equitable, and sustainable society in which all people are accepted as having both the right and the opportunity to work, earn, achieve, and live as self-respecting human beings.

REFERENCES

Adams, Dale W., and Coward, E. Walter, Jr. *Small Farmer Development Strategies.* Seminar Report. Agricultural Development Council. Ohio State Univ., Columbus: Sept. 13–15, 1971.

Balis, John S. *The Utilization of Small Tractors in Integrated Agricultural Development: The Tractor Evaluation Project Applied.* Department of Agricultural Economics, New York State College of Agriculture and Life Sciences, Cornell University, June 1974.

Blue, Richard N., and Weaver, James H. *A Critical Assessment of the Tanzanian Model of Development.* Agricultural Development Council. Reprint no. 30. July 1977.

Dasgupta, Biplab, ed. *Village Studies in the Third World.* Delhi: Hindustan, 1978.

"Dialogue with Asia's Rural Center for the Development of Human Resources in Rural Areas." Pamphlet. Manila.

Dorner, Peter. "International Assistance for the Small Farmer." *Challenge* 18(1975):62–64.

Draft of Declaration of Principles and Programme of Action for World Conference on Agrarian Reform and Rural Development. Food and

Agriculture Organization of the United Nations. New York: March 1979.

Duff, Bart. "The Economics of Small Farm Mechanization in Asia." Paper presented at ORD/ASPAC/FFTC sponsored lecture workshop on the Problems of Small Farm Mechanization, Suweon, Korea, Aug. 12-17, 1977.

El-Abd, Salah. *An Approach to Integrated Rural Development in Africa.* Menoufia, Egypt: Regional Centre for Functional Literacy in Rural Areas for the Arab States, 1973.

Herdt, Robert W., and Barker, Randolph. "Intensification of Proven Farm Production Practices." In *Food Enough or Starvation for Millions,* edited by Douglas Ensminger. New Delhi: Tata McGraw-Hill, 1977.

Ledesma, Antonia L., and Ledesma, Angelita Yap. *Dialogue with Asia's Rural Man.* Report no. 2 of the 1976 CENDHRRA Integral Rural Development Workshops Held in Korea, June 6-13, 1976, and Indonesia, Nov. 7-14, 1976.

Lele, Uma. *The Design of Rural Development: Lessons from Africa.* Baltimore: The Johns Hopkins Univ. Press, 1975.

Lerner, Daniel. *The Passing of Traditional Society: Modernizing the Middle East.* New York: Free Press, 1958.

Nanjundan, S.; Robison, H. E.; and Staley, Eugene. *Economic Research for Small Industry Development.* Bombay: Asia Publishing House, 1962.

Raper, Arthur F. *Rural Development in Action.* Ithaca, N.Y.: Cornell Univ. Press, 1970.

Report of the World Food Council on the Work of its Fourth Session, June 12-15, 1978. General Assembly, United Nations.

Roumasset, James A. *Risk and Uncertainty in Agricultural Development.* Seminar report no. 15. Oct. 1977. Agricultural Development Council.

Wiser, Charlotte V. *Four Families.* Maxwell School of Citizenship and Public Affairs. Syracuse: Syracuse Univ., 1978.

World Bank. *Rural Development.* Sector Policy Paper. Washington, D.C.: Feb. 1975.

World Bank. "Rural Enterprise and Non-Farm Employment." Pamphlet. Jan. 1978.

World Conference on Agrarian Reform and Rural Development. *Review and Analysis of Agrarian Reform and Rural Development in the Developing Countries since the mid-1960s.* FAO, Rome. July 1979.

The World Food Problem. (Proposals for national and international action). United Nations World Food Conference. Rome. Nov. 5-16, 1974.

9

LAND REFORM

Land reform is long overdue and should be given precedence in the poor nations. "Land reform" means an intervention in the prevailing pattern of land ownership, control, and usage to increase productivity and to broaden the distribution of benefits. Land reform, therefore, has deep economic, social, and political implications for many of the poor nations. To accomplish this reform, the individuals who benefit from the present setup will stand to lose a lot of property. It is no wonder that the elite in poor countries are opposed to its implementation.

PATTERNS OF LANDHOLDING AND USE. Patterns of landholding and land use are greatly influenced by political, cultural, climatic, economic, and religious forces.

Experience has shown that political ideologies have a strong influence on the man-land relationship. In general, the right to own, sell, and accumulate land has never been a right for all citizens throughout the world. More often than not, land has been sold at the expense of the public. Some countries, in their quest for equality and justice, regulate the ownership and the right to sell land.

The right to own land is entrusted to the state, and it is the state that organizes and controls land according to a desired objective. In the Republic of South Africa, for example, government control over land has been used to separate the black majority from the white minority, under the guiding policy of apartheid. On the other hand, in the People's Republic of China, rights to land have been designed in such a way as to eliminate rural inequality.

Cultural influence on man-land relationships is also significant. In Ethiopia, land is owned communally in the Governorate General of Begemedir and Semien. The rights to the land are shared collectively based on common descent from "Akni Abat," the founding father who pioneered the area. Members of the extended family have limited rights to use a portion of family land but may not dispose of their portion by gift or sale. Family lands once allocated for an individual's use are generally held by him for life and inherited by his heirs. Because there are many cultures and traditions the world over, there are also many variations in man-land relationships.

In most parts of Africa, land ownership is primarily communal. An African tribal chief is recorded to have remarked that land belongs to a large family, some of whom are dead, some are living, and innumerable others are yet to be born. In East Africa, for example, sedentary agriculture is evident in the temperate areas, while in the more tropical and dry areas shifting cultivation and livestock herding is common. In this case the climatic factor is the dominant determinant.

In poor nations with large rural populations, high population increases, and limited industrialization, land is the most important factor for further growth. In this case, land cannot be viewed as merely a factor of production, since it provides the margin between poverty and subsistence. In industrialized nations, on the other hand, only a small portion of the population is involved in agriculture. Thus the issue of land and land use is not as crucial. The state of a country's development, therefore, plays a significant role in the man-land relationship.

In some poor countries there is little land available for expansion. This is due, in part, to the uneven distribution of land. In addition, it is clear that men's actions and climatic changes in certain areas of the world are turning once productive land into wasteland. During the past half century, on the southern edge of the Sahara alone, about 650,000 square kilometers of land once suitable for agriculture have become barren.

The August 28, 1977, issue of the *New York Times* carried an article by Boyce Rensberger with the headline: "14 Million Acres a Year Vanishing as Deserts Spread around Globe." The article stated:

It is estimated that fertile, productive land is being denuded and destroyed at a rate of 14 million acres a year. Already about 43 percent of the planet's land surface is desert or semidesert.

Unless desertification can be slowed, some scientists say, fully one-third of today's arable land will be lost during the next 25 years, while the world's need for food will nearly double.

POLITICAL IMPLICATIONS. Whichever way the political leaders move today on land and institutional reforms, there will be political tension and a volatile threat of open conflict. To continue supporting the status quo is likely to lead to an eruption from below, resulting in revolution and the overthrow of the government. Legislation to support land and institutional reforms may erode the reformers' political power base and may possibly bring about a change in political leadership as the elite power structure feels threatened.

If governments fail to act on land reform to improve productivity and land distribution, the peasants will, as the man-land ratio worsens. In Mexico, in 1910, Emiliano Zapata led a successful peasant revolution to take over the communal lands occupied by the haciendas. In 1976, riots occurred when there was a change of power. Russia, China, Vietnam, Algeria, and Cuba are countries which have also had similar revolutions.

Yet there can be no general formula for land reform in the developing nations because of the variations in ownership and control from one region to another. Land distribution in terms of farm size varies from one nation to another. Latin American countries have the greatest disparities. Most of the land is held by a few rich individuals. Tenant relationships seem to be common in Asia and the Middle East. However, in Africa, individual land ownership is gaining acceptance, replacing the once common traditional pattern of group ownership and communal rights that still prevails in parts of Ethiopia. In general in the developing countries, new settings have evolved as a result of a break from once common customs or through government (new) action. These changes include private ownership, large plantations, and in the case of socialist oriented countries, state or collective landownership.

POLICIES FOR DEVELOPING COUNTRIES. In general, land reform in most of the developing countries could involve some or all of the following:

1. Redistribution of public or private land to bring about a desired pattern of land distribution and size

2. Consolidation of individual holdings to change the physical pattern of control

3. Change of tenant rights and land ownership, without necessarily redistributing land

4. Change in conditions of tenure upholding security of tenure, equitable crop sharing, and better management

OBSTACLES TO REFORM. The successful implementation of these policies will depend on the political will of the policymakers and the ability of the administration to carry them out. Standing in the way of land reform will be the large landowners, whether they represent the military, religious, or private sectors. To most of the developing countries, land is a symbol of authority and a source of power. Thus land reform will often involve the redistribution of political power as well as wealth. Overly ambitious programs of reform will seldom be successful unless changes in political atmosphere and power are accomplished. Recent experiences show that land reform has been implemented with changes in government in Japan, Mexico, the Republic of China (Taiwan), and Kenya. Effective land reform must mean the abolition of absentee landlordism in whatever form, the setting and enforcing of meaningful ceilings on holdings, and a strict definition of family holdings for owner-cultivators.

INSTITUTIONAL REFORMS. It is important that beneficiaries of land reform be organized before and after its implementation. Institutions must be created that will support the changes. These institutions could insure that land be transferred or that conditions of tenure be altered in accord with the specifications of the reform program. They could also be charged with supplying credit, technical know-how, managerial services, and other essential inputs. Their role would depend on their particular environment. For example, in the case where the landless take up farming for the first time, they would provide short-term and long-term credit as well as technical and managerial service. These institutions could play an important role in bringing about low-cost settlements.

Land reforms without comparable institutional reforms will leave those who become the owner-tillers in a high-risk situation. Without credit institutions oriented to serve all farmers, land tenure legislation will accomplish little. Likewise, extension, research, and marketing institutions should be reformed and oriented to serve all rural people.

The only way to assure farmers that their institutions are there to serve them, is for those institutions to be under their control. Few small farmers in developing countries will risk moving from traditional and subsistence farming to integrating the new technology into their farm plan and family life-style unless there are institutions established and controlled by the small farmers to serve their interests.

When reform programs are implemented, they will abolish larger farms whose owners control services in the agricultural sector. This necessitates long-range planning for services to be provided concurrently with the implementation of reforms. Such an arrangement will minimize costs. In general, the effectiveness of land reform may not be realized immediately. Only in the long run will its benefits be appreciated as they were eventually in Mexico, Japan, Taiwan, and South Korea.

THE MEXICAN EXPERIENCE. Land reform in Mexico goes back to 1915 when land was redistributed to agricultural communities called ejidos. An ejido normally consists of at least twenty individuals, usually family heads and their immediate families. They are supervised and controlled by the Ministry of Agriculture and the National Ejido Bank. The ministry takes care of the day-to-day operations involving the coordination of elections, input of organizational strategies, and the promotion of better agricultural practices. The Ejido Bank, on the other hand, extends credit to the Ejido Cooperative Credit Society. Nor is this all the bank does. It has set up agricultural experiment stations, published technical literature, and investigated agricultural problems.

SMALL FARM STUDIES. Studies carried out by FAO and the World Bank show that small size farm holdings are associated with a higher output per unit of land. Other surveys done in Thailand, the Philippines, Argentina, Brazil, Chile, Colombia, Ecuador, and Guatemala also support FAO and World Bank studies. These findings seem to provide strong support for land reform, which in developing countries would imply smaller landholdings per man. Japan and Taiwan, where farming units are exceedingly small, are among the world's most productive nations in value of output per acre.

The significance of such studies is that reductions in the landholding size or land concentration need not mean a reduction in output per unit of land. This is mainly true because there are limited economies of scale in most agricultural undertakings. Small-farm holders maximize output by applying labor-intensive methods. Actually, large-scale modern agriculture is less productive in resources used than is small-scale agriculture. In developing countries where labor is plentiful, "high output per worker" may be a less valid indicator of efficiency than "output per unit of land" or "output per unit of capital."

The use of more labor on small farms would mean that the output per worker would decrease. The yield per unit would be higher than that of bigger farms but would be shared by an even larger number of families. The net result, however, would be that the land would employ more people and the income generated would be shared more equitably.

Experience shows that marketed surplus declines when big farms are broken up into small landholdings. This happens because small farms tend to consume a greater portion of their output than do larger farms that produce in excess of their own requirements. In India, for example, it has been found that farms 2.5 acres or less sell only 24.5 percent of their output, but farms of 50 acres or more sell 65.4 percent.

If small farms increase significantly in numbers, then the decline in production will be greater. But in general, many poor nations have not been able to produce enough from their big farms to be self-sufficient. Food imports are frequently necessary. As a result, reduction in the size of farms could cause a reduction in the marketed surplus, but the countries could avoid food importation.

JAPAN, TAIWAN, AND SOUTH KOREA. While most new nations early verbalized their concerns about the rural poor and the need for assistance programs for the small farmers and landless laborers, few went beyond political rhetoric. Following World War II, only three countries provided the environment for small farmers to change their values from producing to survive to producing to improve family living. In these countries—Japan, Taiwan, and South Korea—land-reform programs provided incentives for those who tilled the soil to increase production for family gain. All three countries made two of the basic agricultural resources—land and water—more equitably available to all who tilled the soil. And they oriented their agricultural policies to support a better life for the small farmers. They gave priority to the creation of national institutions and services tailored to the small farmers' requirements. Their policies

1. Directed their research establishment to provide agricultural technology oriented to the small farmer
2. Emphasized appropriate technology to introduce mechanical power only where crucial in the farming cycle
3. Emphasized labor-intensive programs
4. Introduced technology to make animal and human labor more productive and human labor less menial and demeaning
5. Stressed the development of price policies and marketing institutions to provide security for the small farmer against losses
6. Tailored educational programs to the needs of small farmers

The small farmers in Japan, Taiwan, and South Korea identified and interacted with the institutional infrastructure purposely developed to serve them. The transition from traditional to modernized agriculture was facilitated. It entailed a movement from the security of past traditions and subsistence production to an identification with and acceptance of new institutions, policies, services, and markets designed for small-farm agriculture.

REFORM CONSIDERATIONS. Land reform should be done with careful consideration. The redistribution of land will depend in large part, on the existing patterns of land distribution and population density. There are countries where population density is so high that without first establishing a minimum acreage, redistribution would produce landholdings of limiting size physically and economically. India and Bangladesh are good examples.

Although land reform must come, legislation for breaking up large landholdings should recognize that if the holdings are too small, the economic and political stability of the country can be permanently damaged. Obviously, the size of the holdings should vary with soil and climate conditions, but they should always be large enough to be an economically viable family farm unit. While making a case for those who till the soil to manage and to reap the harvest from their labor, one should understand that the most equitable land-reform programs cannot give land where none exists. In India, there would still be 20 to 25 million landless laborers.

SMALL FARMER CONSTRAINTS. So we come to the question before us: What constraints keep the small farmer from risking changes in farming practices and family living patterns? Although it would be easy to identify a number of constraints that inhibit the small farmer from moving from traditional to modern agriculture, lack of control over the land he tills and agricultural institutions are the dominant constraints.

Investments in land and water development will benefit only the landholder whose interest is in collecting rent, not the small farmer who is a tenant. The existing land tenure laws in the developing countries in effect provide no incentive for tenants to produce any more than the families' subsistence needs. Obviously, land tenure laws are biased in favor of landlords. Short of land tenure legislation transferring ownership to those who till the soil, security of tenancy, and rental arrangements providing incentives for tenants to put in extra investments and labor should be considered.

PLANNING. Planning will be of signal importance when implementing land reforms. The people must be educated. Implementation must be timed to minimize disruption of the agricultural process as a whole. For example, redistribution of land either just before planting or during harvest will cause problems.

One serious impediment to effective planning of land reform programs is the attitude that small and marginal farmers warrant a low priority in agricultural planning because they do not contribute to the market surplus. Yet the framework for these schemes continues to be market-oriented. Unless there is a fundamental change in planning attitudes, the small farmers will remain underprivileged. Furthermore, the magnitude of the food deficit developing countries will face in 1986 is expressed as a market demand (of 85 to 110 million), rather than in terms of human needs.

Apparently it is time to examine all forms of group farming as alternatives to the present tenure arrangements, given the production limitations of small holdings, the large number of destitute, landless laborers, and the exploitation of tenants by landlords in developing countries. While significant lessons can be drawn from the forms of organization in Israel, the People's Republic of China, Tanzania, Yugoslavia, and Taiwan, each country will have to design its own innovative approach, one that promises to work under the country's own cultural, political, and economic circumstances.

New or alternative forms of organization with which the small landholders, landless laborers, and exploited tenants can identify are essential or poverty in rural areas will persist, and food-crop agriculture will fail to respond to the national and nutritional requirements of the people.

ALTERNATIVE FARMING SYSTEMS

Small-Farm Agriculture. The key sector in developing countries in determining both the quantity and quality of food that will be available in the future for human consumption is small-farm agriculture, which is mostly food-crop agriculture. Thus the focus should be on the smallest of the small farms and their special needs for appropriate technology and institutions to direct and support farm enterprises and cropping systems. The immediate need is for research to determine what kinds of crops and farm enterprises will return the greatest net income and provide greater security within climatic variabilities to the "one-to-five-acre farmer." Yet research without institutions oriented to the farmers' acceptance of the recommended cropping and farming systems will not result in the application of the new technology.

Although enhancing the earnings and assuring access to irrigation must be regarded as immediate concerns, priority should be given to the one-to-five-acre farms in the dry, rain-fed areas. These are the farmers whose return from land is the lowest, whose risks are the greatest, and whose poverty is most intense.

Cropping systems and the identification of the range of crops that can be grown within a specific region by soil types and within climatic constraints should merit first emphasis. Furthermore, within climatic constraints, a determination must be made of how many different crops can be grown on a given piece of land within one year or growing season. Finally, a complementary combination of crops to be included in an intercropping system must be established.

Answers to these questions will require the work of interdisciplinary research teams. For example, the plant breeder can be expected to breed for varieties that will mature within the time period required for a multicropping system. The agronomist must find an answer to tillage practices for both multicropping and intertillage systems. The weed control specialist should test the use of herbicides to control weeds as a substitute to cultivation. The entomologist must develop a pesticide control program for intertillage cropping systems. The agricultural engineer will have to develop appropriate animal-drawn implements for both multiplecropping and intercropping systems.

Since the objective of developing a farming system is to maximize net income in addition to the development of both intercropping systems, there should be research on livestock (cattle, sheep, and goats), poultry, beekeeping, and fish culture. Special emphasis should be given to dairying. When all essential conditions are met, a one-to-five-acre farmer can make a good living, earn enough to provide for a nutritional diet, and meet basic family needs through a combination of one or two good dairy cows and a cropping and farming system.

A feasibility study should be a prior condition for making policy decisions on the introduction of cropping and farming systems in an area. This study should provide answers to a number of questions, the more important being: What will be the economics of carrying out the recommended cropping and farming system? Will the profit margin be sufficient to motivate the family to accept the additional work and will it cover the risk? Do markets for the projected farm produce presently exist or will they have to be developed? What additional institutions and services will be needed for farmers to carry out the recommended cropping and farming system? Assuming the feasibility study recommendations are economically sound and have the potential for increasing the small farmers' income and economic security, the farmers' acceptance of the recommended cropping and farming system must be based on a time schedule and operational plans for development of both markets and all the supporting institutions and services. Without the markets and the supporting institutions and services, the recommendations will and should be rejected by the small farmers.

Home Garden Programs. Since policies of the developing countries have not included programs to integrate the landless laborers and small landholders into the countries' socioeconomy, the innovative developmental strategy now proposed for landless laborers and holders of small units is a home garden program (fruits and vegetables) to meet family nutritional needs and economic enterprises to provide needed supplementary income. The short term objective is to provide these two population groups with the quantity and quality of food for minimal nutritional requirements, thus freeing them from the fear of hunger, as well as providing opportunities to earn money. The long-term strategy should be to increase production sufficiently to have food to market in excess of family nutritional needs.

A home garden program for the landless laborers and small landholders should make it possible to change what Diogenes, the Greek philosopher, replied when asked about the proper time to eat. He observed, "If a rich man, when you will; if a poor man, when you can."

The first essential action to make a home garden program succeed will be to implement national policies providing landless laborers with a unit of land large enough to produce all the fruits and vegetables for the nutritional needs of a family of five to six people. The size of the land unit will depend on rainfall and climatic conditions. When the present small holdings are not large enough for an adequate size garden unit, additional land should be allocated.

The land to be assigned through nontransferable leases to landless laborers for their family gardens can come from four sources: community and village land, government land, land reform legislation, and cooperatives funded by the government to purchase blocks of land to be subdivided into garden units.

The home garden program will require government support for

research, a special extension staff, and special institutional services. This is similar to the way the large farm, market-oriented sector of the economy is served by government funded research, extension, and institutional services. A garden program would fail without the institutional services and the development of the new technology for producing fruits and vegetables.

At the outset, cooperatives at the community and village level should be accepted as having an important role to play in a home garden program. Initially, the community and village cooperative should provide custom services and should organize and manage a water supply for irrigation. The local cooperative could borrow money to drill a well, dig a pond, or construct a dam to provide water for irrigation.

Obviously, water will play a crucial role in a home garden program. Therefore, a national program should be started in areas where water is available. Where it is not, priority should be granted for the development of water sources for irrigation. Expansion of the home garden program should proceed as rapidly as reliable sources of water for irrigation permit.

A national program to consolidate small fragmented landholdings into one block of land would make irrigation of this land feasible. Surplus land that accrues from consolidation should be added to this block of land and then assigned to landless laborers for home gardens.

Later, when it is appropriate to begin planning to implement the long-term strategy of producing some foods for the market in excess of the family nutritional needs, the local cooperative should serve as a reliable marketing institution. These cooperatives could also foster local food processing industries.

The introduction of home garden programs into rural economies will be a difficult and formidable task. The program should provide both the quantity and quality of food to meet the minimum nutritional needs of landless laborers. But the difficulties in gaining acceptance of this program cannot be overstated. This plan will be running against the cultural grain and present preferences for single cereal diets. Yet if this seems an impossible task, it should be remembered that in the past thirty years the revolutionary land and institutional reforms to make the production resources more equitably available seemed even more impossible to achieve.

National leadership must be at the cabinet level, since the home garden program will focus on the two largest poverty groups in the rural areas and involve millions of family units. Either a special deputy minister in the ministry of agriculture should be designated, or in large countries such as India, a new ministry for home gardens should be created. A program administered by the present ministers of agriculture, whose commitments are to large-farm, market-oriented agriculture, will be at a competitive disadvantage for the requisite leadership time and for financial and institutional support.

An imaginative home garden program for the millions of landless laborers and the holders of small units would have worldwide appeal for governments, institutions, and individuals who are seeking to eliminate world hunger and poverty. The governments that provide food aid could assign the generated local currencies to a home garden program. Institutions, especially churches, would find raising funds for a home garden program appealing. Peace Corps workers would find a home garden program tailor-made for them to play a useful role. CARE seed and garden tool packages would be relevant and useful.

RURAL ECONOMIC ENTERPRISES. Food-crop and livestock agriculture alone cannot provide employment for all the landless laborers and artisans. There should be a national program for creating economic enterprises in the rural areas. Thus economic enterprises, along with food-crop and livestock agriculture, should provide the primary employment opportunities for landless laborers and artisans, but they should also become a secondary source of income for the very small landholders.

Rural enterprises should stengthen the economic base and provide continuity in employment opportunities. As a consequence, great care should be exercised in selecting rural enterprises, and the criteria for loaning money to start these enterprises should be based on their potential economic viability.

Extension Institutes. Institutions to service the program are of primary importance, but in addition there must be regional research, training, and extension institutes. The number of rural enterprise institutes will depend on the size of the country and its population distribution. These regional institutes should have an economic analysis unit to provide guidance in the selection of enterprises to be funded. The research division should concentrate on equipment design and the layout required to produce a quality product at a competitive price. The research division should be innovative in design and adapted to local conditions. The extension division should be highly mobile, able to move into rural areas to work directly with rural enterprises.

Banks. Important to the process of creating economic growth and thereby increasing employment opportunities will be the early inception of several interrelated enterprises. Initially, priority should be given to enterprises that will foster agricultural development. The expansion of agriculture should be reflected in a commensurate increase in purchasing power.

A bank in the center village or growth center will play a significant role. It should make an all-out appeal to the people to deposit their savings, and through liberal loan policies it should actively promote economic enterprises.

Rural enterprises involving small industries, dairying, sheep-raising, fisheries, beekeeping, handlooming, blacksmithing, food processing, and chicken hatcheries for selling eggs can be included. The enterprises can be individually owned, or they can be cooperatives for processing, storage, or marketing. The rural-based enterprise can manufacture parts as a subsidiary of a large urban-based industry. Opening rural industrial estates to provide water and electricity will encourage and facilitate the starting of new enterprises.

Councils. While national leadership and strong political commitment for a rural economic enterprise program will be important, the participation of the people through local rural enterprise councils will be the determining factor for success. These rural enterprise councils should be elected bodies. To be effective, the local councils must be recognized as the official body to provide leadership for development.

SUMMARY. Although it may be a drawn-out process beset with many false starts, it seems a safe prediction that as political leaders examine their alternatives, they will conclude their best choice of survival will be in looking to the rural poor as the most likely power base for their future and will, therefore, support land and institutional reforms. While a case can be made for far-reaching land and institutional reforms as a condition for achieving a more egalitarian society, it is important to bear in mind that the needed reforms can only be carried out by the countries themselves.

There is reason to hope that developing countries will give greater priority to legislation implementing land reforms in the decade of the eighties. The basis for this renewed optimism is to be found in the July 12–20, 1979 Rome World Conference on Agrarian Reform and Rural Development. This conference, sponsored by the FAO of the United Nations, made the following proposals for land reform in a draft declaration of principles and programs of action:

II. ACCESS TO LAND, WATER AND OTHER RESOURCES

Ownership and use of land and access to water and other natural productive resources are key determinants of rural economic structures, income distribution and general conditions of rural life. Where these structures are judged to be constraints on rural development and the achievement of social equity, governments should consider institutional and policy changes within the context of their national and rural development goals.

A. Reorganization of Land Tenure

In countries where substantial land redistribution is part of the rural development strategy, the government should consider action to:

(i) Acquire land, water and other natural resources at a price or other type of compensation which is fair and equitable in relation to the value of assets and to the economic capacity and resources of the country.

(ii) Give precedence in the distribution of assets thus acquired to established tenants, smallholders and agricultural workers with particular attention to the most deprived groups.

(iii) Implement redistribution with speed and determination to avert disinvestment and evasive transfers.

(iv) Create and support post-reform institutions with the widest feasible participation of the beneficiaries to prevent the emergence of new patterns of concentration of resources or other forms of exploitation.

B. Tenancy Reform and Regulation of Rural Wages

Where substantial redistribution of land and other assets is not part of a country's strategy, the government should consider action to:

(i) Introduce and/or effectively enforce legal measures to ensure rent ceilings fair to tenants combined with security of tenure.

(ii) Encourage the formation of tenants' organizations to promote group solidarity, supervise the implementation of regulatory measures and enhance the ability of tenants to seek legal redress.

(iii) Establish and enforce minimum wage standards to protect rural workers from exploitation.

C. Regulation of Changes in Customary Tenure

Where a country's strategy includes changes in customary tenure systems, governments should consider action to:

(i) Arrest trends toward unequal privatization of rights and absentee ownership and protect the rights of small cultivators.

(ii) Preserve and adapt, or where necessary create, systems of broad-based community control and management of land and water rights in accordance with development needs.

D. Land Consolidation and the Promotion of Group Farming

In countries where efficient production is hindered by severe fragmentation of holdings, governments should consider action to:

(i) Intensify efforts to consolidate fragmented holdings to improve productivity and management.

(ii) Wherever appropriate, combine consolidation measures with programmes of community-wide and area-wide development.

(iii) Encourage group farming and common management of grazing lands.

E. Community Control Over Natural Resources

In countries where the public domain includes substantial forests, range lands and water resources, governments should consider action to:

(i) Arrange for control and management of such resources in the public interest and consistent with environmental conservation.

(ii) Ensure equitable access to natural resources in the public domain and promote better utilization.

F. Settlement of Unoccupied Public Lands

In countries where a significant land frontier exists, the government should consider action to:

(i) Promote settlement on new land of the largest feasible number of landless households and provide the necessary infrastructure and services to ensure their success.

(ii) Ensure that such schemes will be supplementary to, not a substitute for, agrarian reforms necessary in already settled areas.

REFERENCES

Dumont, Rene. *False Start in Africa,* 2d ed. New York: Praegar Publishers, 1969.

Klatt, W. "Causes and Cures of Agrarian Unrest in Asia," *Southeast Asian Spectrum* 3(1974):7–8.

Svobida, Lawrence. *An Empire of Dust.* Caldwell, Idaho: Caxton Printers, 1940.

United Nations Research Institute for Social Development. "Organization of Land Redistribution Beneficiaries," Report no. 70.1, Geneva, 1970.

World Bank Paper "Land Reform." Rural Development Series, 1974.

10

PERSONAL DEVELOPMENT

There is reason for hope today that as the quality of life emerges as a national objective, developing countries will examine their options and the implications of the widening gap between the elite and the poor. As development increasingly emphasizes removing the conditions that create poverty and improving the quality of life, it will be consistent with those objectives to think positively about transforming the educational system to stress the development of people as human beings with respect for self.

EDUCATION

Purposes. The emphasis is on transforming the present educational system, not merely modifying or making minor changes in it. To transform an educational system concerned primarily with developing self-reliant people can be done either through formal or informal education. Its main purpose should be to transmit from one generation to the next the accumulative knowledge and wisdom of society and to prepare young people for future membership in that society. Present educational systems are inappropriately formal. In developing countries where traditional values are dominant, informal education will be more relevant in preparing children to grow up and function in society. Formal education presently alienates those from the rural cultures who go through primary and secondary schools. They are educated to leave the village and rural community, thus abandoning the people in the community.

Time factor. There should be no illusions about the difficult and time-consuming efforts required of people to develop as self-respecting human beings. Time, measured in decades, and participation on a basis of equality of opportunity, will be required to create communities capable of improving the quality of life for all. The values of interdependence and a sense of belonging and caring for the community emerge only through time and through working together.

Impact on Farmers. Because the primary source of livelihood in the rural areas is agriculture, the new educational system must produce good farmers. Education should prepare everyone in a free society to be responsible and responsive citizens. People must think for themselves. They must understand problems, weigh alternative solutions, make decisions, and act in accord with those decisions. Illiteracy, ignorance, and acceptance of an inferior status have no place in a free society. For that society to remain free and open, all people should be competent to judge issues and be motivated to work toward a society where all are equal.

Need for Transformation. There are no alternatives to transforming the primary and secondary schools as they are presently structured and functioning, since a new educational system cannot be adapted from the colonially imposed educational system. Therefore, it is possible but not yet predictable that the time is approaching when the developing countries can and will accept the need for revolutionary reforms in education. Like all revolutions, leadership for change must come from within the countries. But before basic changes in educational systems can take place, a clear and forceful statement of the country's national development objectives and an answer to the question, Education for what purpose? is needed.

WOMEN AND DEVELOPMENT. Rural women are potentially the most valuable resource in planning and implementing rural programs, including agriculture, health, family planning, nutrition, and quality of life. As they become involved in planning and implementing development programs, they will have a more direct and consistent concern about the quality of rural life.

Cultural Roles. As mothers, women play a dominant role in molding character and in transmitting cultural values to their children. Thus women must become better educated, and better informed through their participation in all phases of development. As informed and educated mothers, they will play a major role in preparing their children for change while maintaining values important to their culture.

Food Production. In their maternal role, women are the socializers of the next generation. In recognition of the important role of women in food production throughout the developing countries, the 1974 United Nations Rome Food Conference passed the following resolution:

Considering that the major part of the required increase in food production must occur in the developing countries if the present tragedy of starvation and malnutrition for uncounted millions is not to continue,

Recognizing that rural women in the developing world account for at least fifty percent of food production,

Knowing that women everywhere generally play the major role in procurement and preparation of food consumed by their families,

Recognizing the important role of the mother in the health development of future generations through proper lactation and, furthermore, that mothers in most cultures are the best source of food for their very young children,

Reaffirming the importance of the World Health Assembly resolution on lactation in May this year,

1.   Calls on all Governments to involve women fully in the decision-making machinery for food production and nutrition policies as part of a total development strategy;

2.   Calls on all Governments to provide to women in law and in fact the right to full access to all medical and social services, particularly special nutritious food for mothers and the means to space their children to allow maximum lactation, as well as education and information essential to the nurture and growth of mentally and physically healthy children;

3.   Calls on all Governments to include in their plan provision for education and training for women on an equal basis with men in food production and agricultural technology, marketing and distribution techniques, as well as to put at their disposal consumer, credit, and nutrition information;

4.   Calls on all Governments to promote equal rights and responsibilities for men and women in order that the energy, talent and ability of women can be fully utilized in partnership with men in the battle against world hunger.

Factors Determining Women's Roles. The varied roles women play are influenced by cultural and socioeconomic factors. Since a nation's stage of development has a bearing on the role of women, developing nations differ from the West in this respect. At least three factors influence variations in the role of women:

1. Specialization of labor is associated with social and economic development in the farming societies of the world. This division is on a sex basis and is widely accepted.

2. Basically two types of subsistence agriculture are performed under this simple division of labor: one in which women are responsible for most of the food production with little help from men; and the other where men are responsible for food production with little assistance from women.

3. In other fields women seem to be occupied primarily in a narrow range of traditional occupations, although this traditional setup is being challenged in many parts of the world by women's liberation movements. The degree of acceptability depends on the society. In the West, changes have been rapid, while in developing countries they are slow.

The African System. In Africa the role of women is very important. The growing of food in many parts of Africa is women's responsibility. Where shifting cultivation is practiced, men cut the trees and clear the land. Then women, with the traditional hoe, prepare the soil, plant, weed, and harvest the crop.

In many parts of Africa the dominance of women in agriculture predates colonization. When Europeans first went into Africa they were surprised to find women dominating farming, and their immediate reaction was to try to get men to take over. They induced the male population to produce cash crops by imposing a poll tax. In some instances, however, the colonialists expanded the role of women in agriculture by forcefully or voluntarily involving men in other activities such as road building, construction work, and mining. But these activities included a very small portion of the male labor force.

The impact of the colonial activities in Africa has been to further institutionalize the role of women in agriculture. In most cases women are in charge of food-crop farming. In a few cases, work is shared with men. But there are also cases where men dominate, especially in the production of cash crops.

Colonial rule in Africa contributed to increasing differences in the agricultural productivity between male and female because the new techniques of farming were made available to men, but not to women. Men also had access to the new types of equipment while women still struggled with such traditional methods as the hoe.

The importance of cash crops to the colonial powers as earners of foreign exchange led to research and other government investments in cash crops which were produced by men. Until recently, women's work, primarily concerned with food-crop production, received little support. Furthermore, the earnings from cash crops were used by men to improve their production; yet the women who produced to feed the family did not have the resources to expand or improve production practices.

The practice of polygamy in Africa is crucial to the support of agriculture. A man with several wives normally commands more land, produces more food, and gains higher status. Polygamy functions as an integral part of the economic system and it plays a significant role in areas where land for expansion is available.

While it is the women who do most of the farming in Africa, men own the land. Land is passed from father to son in the patrilinear tribes, and from mother to daughter in matrilinear tribes. Land is seldom sold. However, when land is sold it will most likely end up in the hands of the men rather than women because men have money from their cash crops or wages from direct labor. Thus landownership tends to concentrate in the hands of men.

The Asian System. A totally different work pattern is present in the Asian farming system. First of all, this region is characterized by the common use of the plow. It is used with the help of animals, and some of the hand operations are left to women. Here women's role in agriculture varies with subcultures and crops. Men prepare the land and maintain it, while women weed, harvest, and tend the farm animals.

Another common feature of the Asian system is the existence of private landownership and a large number of landless families. This differs from the African system, where land is communally owned and private ownership is not as strong. In Asia, the use of paid farm labor is very common and involves both men and women.

In India the caste system presents a special framework for labor. The "high-caste" women do not take part in farming activities. The next caste below is characterized by women involved in domestic affairs. The third group consists of women who help their husbands in the fields. In the lowest caste, both men and women are engaged in farm work for a living. They are constantly seeking jobs to feed their families.

Discrimination in Development Assistance. When one examines development assistance in agriculture, including extension education, it becomes apparent that all agricultural programs are focused on men. Men are trained for the kinds of tasks that women do. It must be accepted that in addition to providing services and organizing extension programs, it will take time to change what has become traditional. What is important is the growing recognition that in the future, programs must be organized to serve women's roles in food production. Women's involvement in all decisions related to farming must be accepted.

Past development strategies to modernize agriculture in the developing countries will tend to reduce the role of women, since women are and have been used traditionally for hand operations. Progress in modernizing agriculture will depend on population trends and on developing nations' ability to acquire capital, which in the past has been a big problem. As a result, capital-intensive methods will be less attractive. If this is the case, then the role of women could be expanded.

Cultural Values. Cultural values greatly influence the role of women in agriculture. For example, Milik Ashraf in an article on "Notes on the Role of Rural Pakistani Women in Farming in the Northwest Frontier Province" (*Land Tenure News,* 1977) comments:

Because of traditional Islamic values, the location of the farm job is an important variable influencing participation of women. According to these customs, women are not expected to be seen barefaced outside their homes. There is a division of labor between men and women: Men doing the field jobs and women contributing to farm jobs which can be done inside the family compound or which relate to care of livestock and, in some areas only, on jobs involving fieldwork.

In Vietnam (see Dana Raphael, ed., *Being Female: Reproduction, Power, and Change,* 1975):

A wife is the center of the household. It is she who is constantly caring for the family, influencing the husband, caring for the finances, and doing whatever benefits the family group. Her role is to pay formal respect to her husband, to his family and ancestors as well as her own, to continue her virtuous way of life so that she brings no shame to either family, and to produce children, especially sons. A husband has great freedom to come and go at will. This leaves the woman the major authority within the family. Like daughters, wives use indirect persuasion and exert 'gentle pressure' to control their husbands, and this can sometimes include threatened or real attempts at self-destruction.

In countries like Ghana (see Alice Schelgel, ed., *Sexual Stratification: A Cross Cultural View,* 1977):

. . . where women traditionally enjoyed relatively high status, the social changes accompanying modernization may in the long run undermine the position of women, and particularly their role in the family, even more than they reduce their economic options. In terms of affecting the quality of life and the future possibilities for redressing the present imbalance in the sex-role division, this social devaluation and weakening of women's roles may have even more profound repercussions than women's impaired access to opportunities in the modern sector.

Planning Strategies. The absence of women in planning and development for the past thirty years has led to an emphasis on economic growth and materialistic values. Absent in planning and development strategies is any focus on the nation's valuable human resources. Programs to improve the quality of life for all people were never central to five-year plans and national objectives. When the environment became a popular concern in the late sixties, five-year plans stressed environmental impact on development. The emphasis is now shifting to women's impact on development.

One of the most important changes to have surfaced in development policies in the past thirty years has been the acceptance of the potentially strategic role of women in development. Leaders of developing countries' programs for aid assistance and agencies for international development are now stressing the involvement of women in all phases of development. However, it would be naive to assume that those who now accept the role of women in development do so because they believe women have a major contribution to make. Women's role in development is now the "in thing." No one wants to be against such a widely accepted new development strategy.

Political Commitment. There are wide differences in intellectual and political commitments to involve women in development. Without a deep political commitment, backed by political institutional support, such major national programs as agriculture and family planning contribute little to change. And the strength of any political commitment to women's involvement in development is yet to be tested. The new consensus that they be brought into the development process is an important first step. The new development strategy involves women in all phases of development, offers greater emphasis on the development of people as human beings, and promotes institutions and programs that contribute to improving the quality of life for all people.

Actually, it is hard to make a case for the exclusion of women in these plans. Certain areas stand out as ones that would benefit by including women in strategies and planning. On the national level, women have a contribution to make by defining national objectives, selecting development strategies for specific programs, and allocating resources to implement programs. At the rural community level, women can help define rural development objectives, diagnose problems, establish priorities, and examine alternative development strategies.

Program Areas. Specific program areas where women must be included are: family-life agriculture, rural enterprises, health, nutrition, family planning, education, rural organizations and institutions, and family quality-of-life programs.

Since women play a major role in maintaining family values that perpetuate traditional ways of thinking, behaving, living, and family work patterns, they should be able to influence the acceptance of new attitudes in these areas. Yet effective planning and development programs involving women must begin with their education and development as human beings. There is a great difference between "using" women to enhance development and in educating and nurturing the growth of women as human beings. Without first providing for the education and personal growth of women, programs merely to involve women in development will not draw on their full potential.

With the shift from food to allay hunger to food to meet nutritional needs, women must be educated to understand how a nutritionally adequate diet contributes to family health and meets the energy requirement of the family members. It will be necessary to either create new research institutions or strengthen existing ones to support essential nutritional education programs.

For women to be accepted as equals to men and as full partners in development, educational programs must change women's traditional role from mother to human being with interests and achievements in many areas. As long as the culture remains ignorant of women's potential, family planning will run counter to cultural values. Education of the female child is probably the single most important factor in decreasing the birthrate. If they are educated, they will be knowledgeable and trained to achieve status in other areas besides motherhood.

The cultural value of subsisting to survive must be changed before the family will respond to programs to improve the quality of family life. Women should be included in the leadership that formulates and carries out programs designed to improve the quality of family life. And the traditional family must find in these programs a new sense of security. Understandably, families hold tenaciously to traditional ways because they minimize their risks. Therefore, quality-of-life programs must take account of existing values, and they must have built into them proven alternative ways of living and earning that minimize risk. The mere announcement of programs to improve the quality of family life will be ineffective. What is needed is a demonstration of alternatives that will work, presented in a way that can be grasped by the people.

Rural enterprises must provide women with alternatives to their presently limited opportunities for contributing to the income of their families. It is the first step in improving the family level of living. In the absence of rural economic enterprises, women's work is both tedious and limited because of meager production resources. Again, education of women becomes central to their role in the development of economic enterprises as well as contributing to their success.

The presently limited formal education of women is a handicap to development; they ought to be brought into the arena now. Girls must have an equal opportunity with boys to primary and secondary education immediately. Political leaders should support women's involvement in development and assure girls of educational training to understand problems, to weigh alternative strategies, and to leadership involving change but preserving cultural identity.

If we are to see an improvement in the quality of life and personal development of the masses now living in poverty, policies and programs must be enacted to establish a just and equal society, concerned with the enlightenment and education of all women and men in the socioeconomic spectrum. Educated women in the developing countries can understand the relationship between nutrition and good health. As informed mothers, they can nurture the citizens of the future and influence and share the leadership in transforming traditional societies.

REFERENCES

Ashraf, Milik. "Notes on the Role of Rural Pakistani Women in Farming in the Northwest Frontier Province." *Land Tenure Center News.* Univ. of Wisconsin-Madison, No. 55, Jan.–Mar. 1977.

Cleveland, Harlan, and Wilson, Thomas W., Jr. *Human Growth: An Essay on Growth, Values and the Quality of Life.* Princeton: Aspen Institute for Humanistic Studies, 1978.

Coombs, Philip H., and Manzoon, Ahmed. *Attacking Rural Poverty: How Nonformal Education Can Help.* Baltimore: The Johns Hopkins Univ. Press, 1974.

Raphael, Dana, ed. *Being Female: Reproduction, Power, and Change.* The Hague: Mouton, 1975.

Report of the World Food Conference, Rome, Nov. 5-16, 1974. New York: United Nations, 1975.

Schlegel, Alice. *Sexual Stratification: Cross Cultural View* (sup. 96). New York: Columbia Univ. Press, 1977.

Tinker, Irene, and Bramsen, Michele Bo, eds. *Women and World Development.* New York: Praeger, 1976.

Ward, Champion F., ed. *Education and Development Reconsidered: The Bellagio Conference Papers.* New York: Praeger, 1974.

"Women and Development," *Report,* July-Aug. 1977.

11

IN THREE GENERATIONS

Running through the book have been major interrelated strands: removing conditions that create poverty and providing all with an opportunity to work, earn, and achieve; developing self-respecting human beings; developing institutions to serve everyone; improving the quality of life, especially for the laborers, artisans, tenants, and small landholders; fostering political commitment and leadership; creating strategies for change; integrating the rural poor into the national socioeconomic and political fabric; and providing the necessary time to transform traditional societies into modern societies utilizing science and technology.

The case has been made that hunger has become a world concern, rising at times to crisis dimensions. People can be expected to have food enough for minimum nutritional needs only when the 850 million to 1 billion people living in poverty gain access to production and institutional resources. Hunger is the child of poverty, and poverty results from the denial of opportunities to work, earn, and achieve.

The emerging adult populations were children during the decades when developing countries gained independence. They come into adulthood knowing that they no longer have to live as their parents did under colonial rule. The parents of this emerging generation will caution them against the risks of accepting all that is new.

The grandchildren of the adults at the time of independence are now being born. They will grow up in the midst of change, and when they reach adulthood, change will be a part of their way of life.

The adults at the time of independence constitute today's decision makers. They, with their parents, continue to be the guardians of cultural values and traditions. Moreover, survival has demanded a strict adherence to traditions. Thus the present adults are basically traditionalists, but they have been motivated over the past thirty years through education, demonstrations, and persuasion to accept many new ways of doing things. But in their attitudes, they will remain traditionalists for the remainder of their lives.

To complete the cultural transformation from traditionalism to modernism in three generations, the education of the children of the present adult population and their descendants must be oriented toward better preparation for earning a living and toward more effective living within their environment.

Since all development takes place through people and their institutions, the conclusion is inevitable that improvement in the quality of life for all can be achieved only as the beneficiaries grow in respect for themselves as human beings. They must also be directly involved through organizations and institutions in all phases of the development process.

Finally, while many factors condition the development process, the two dominant factors are political commitment and organizing the rural poor for economic advancement and social achievement.

Again and again, the analysis points up the necessity of understanding the span of time required as well as the actual process involved in transforming traditional societies, which may take as long as three generations. There should be no mystery about the changes required to integrate the poor majority into the national socioeconomic and political fabric and to move them toward a modernized society.

The time span, three human generations, represents about sixty-five years. The present adult population in the developing countries is completing the first generation of transition. This generation has been exposed to great changes in their movement from colonial status to statehood. They have progressed from a colonial policy, supporting the status quo, to an era of far-reaching changes.

Education for self-reliance should recognize people's dependence on effective organizations and institutions over which they should dominate. When today's children become the decision makers, they will rely increasingly on science and technology to devise alternative solutions. But they will be held back by their parents and grandparents from completely disregarding traditional values and traditional ways of living and earning a living.

Only when the grandchildren of the adult population at the time of independence become adults and decision makers will one see people capable of trusting science, technology, and institutions in much the same way as the adults today place their trust in traditionalism.

To provide a reference point in helping to understand the time and process involved in transforming traditional societies, a search was made of religious literature and the following is presented as an example of generational change.

"The Exodus," A Model of Cultural Change

There are many stories of cultural change and social transformation within the traditional and religious literature of the world's peoples. The biblical story of the Exodus from Egypt and wanderings in the desert of the Hebrew people is one of these traditional accounts of the process of cultural change. It reflects an understanding that the process is not only time consuming but is marked by setbacks and moments of dramatic transformation.

The story opens with the Hebrews living under oppression in Egypt where the Egyptians made ruthless use of them as slaves in every kind of hard labor. Yet even under these conditions, the people were reluctant to support Moses when he appeared as a leader offering them freedom and their own land. Part of the reason for this resistance was fear of their Egyptian overlords; but it is also reasonable to see here an indication that people, particularly those whose existence is marginal, prefer the security of the known to the risk of change. The implied message is, "This life may be hard, but I am alive and I at least know what to expect. If I try to change and fail, I may lose what little I have."

After the escape from Egypt, the Bible records a period of more than forty years in the wilderness during which the people underwent a cultural transformation from polytheism to monotheism, from slavery to self-governing tribes, received a new legal code, and developed their own social and cultural patterns. (Most of the last half of Exodus, and the books of Leviticus and Deuteronomy, record the traditional understanding of this process and the legal, religious, and social codes they eventually produce.) However, this process was not a smooth one. Moments of exhilaration and triumph were followed by periods of challenge and despair. From the very beginning, there were accounts of grumbling, resistance to change, and a desire to return to the old way—slavery and all.

It is interesting to note that most of these periods of rebellion related to anxiety about food, while the others expressed fears of the unknown. At the very time that Moses was receiving the Ten Commandments from God at the top of Mount Sinai, the people gathered below lapsed into despair and idolatry. Perhaps there is a lesson for our times here. No matter how great the vision of a group's leaders,

Special thanks to Dr. W. Douglas Ensminger, Pastor, Parkside Presbyterian Church, Madison, Wisconsin, for having researched the religious literature and written the final section of this book.

proposals for cultural change will meet with misunderstanding and resistance. And especially after a dramatic change, some backlash yearning for the traditional ways should be expected.

This traditional account of a process of cultural change also testifies to the fact that the process cannot take place within a single generation and cannot be rushed. Within a few years of their escape from Egypt, the Hebrews reached the edge of the Promised Land and sent out spies to explore the land. The spies returned with a mixed message—the land is very rich, "flowing with milk and honey . . . but its inhabitants are sturdy, and the cities are strongly fortified." Once again, on the verge of a major breakthrough, the people despaired and rebelled against their leaders. Because of their rebellion, it was decreed that none of that fearful generation would be allowed to enter the Promised Land. While the story is told as one of Divine Judgment, it is also a parable about the pace of social change. If you try to make people move too far, too fast, they will not be able to absorb the changes and will rebel. Major change takes generations, not merely years.

To bring about the cultural transformation of the developing countries' traditional societies, to remove the conditions that create poverty, to develop people as human beings having respect for self, to integrate the rural poor into the socioeconomic and political fabric of the nation, and to improve the level of living of all people—if this can be done in three generations—it will be the greatest achievement of this century.

REFERENCES

Advance Through Crisis. Democracy in Action: No. 7 New York: Council for Democracy, 1941.

Bennis, Warren G.; Benne, Kenneth D.; and Chin, Robert, eds. *The Planning of Change*. New York: Holt, Rinehart, and Winston, 1962.

Gore, M. S., ed. *Problems of Rural Change: Some Case Studies*. Delhi: Delhi School of Social Work, 1963.

Wiser, Charlotte V. *Four Families*. Maxwell School of Citizenship and Public Affairs. Syracuse: Syracuse Univ., 1978.

INDEX